Andrew Wyeth · Boston Museum

Distributed by New York Graphic Society · Greenwich, Connecticut

Museum of Fine Arts, Boston

ANDREW WYETH

Introduction by David McCord

Selection by Frederick A. Sweet

Library of Congress Catalogue Card No. 75-127419. ISBN 0-87846-051-9.
Type set in Linofilm Palatino and Trump Gravure by Wrightson Typographers, Boston
Color separations by Vario Color Separators under the supervision of Harry Lerner
Printed in the United States of America by The Meriden Gravure Company, Meriden, Connecticut
Designed by Carl F. Zahn

JACKET ILLUSTRATION:

113 *SEASHELLS. Dry brush, 1953, 11 5/16 x 15 5/16 in.*
   Lent by Mrs. Andrew Wyeth
Just empty mussel shells caught in the sand, but their faded blue appears again and again
in Wyeth's work. Beside his easel is a flat dish full of shells he has picked up on the
islands or even found in the middle of the woods. They are not perfect or rare shells, but
to him their color has meaning.

Foreword

Ever since the late connoisseur-collector, Stephen C. Clark, stopped in at the Macbeth Gallery on Fifty-seventh Street one day in 1948, saw *Christina's World* and bought it for the Museum of Modern Art, Andrew Wyeth's reputation has advanced with increasing speed so that today he is the most famous living American painter and surely the most loved. It would be as easy to state as well that *Christina's World* is the most familiar painting by an American artist alive today. Various reasons have been advanced to account for Wyeth's popularity, none of them entirely satisfactory. Perhaps a lesson can be drawn from another American artist in another era.

The Museum of Fine Arts was founded one hundred years ago, in 1870. If one could have asked the founding fathers to name the most popular American artist of that day, without doubt the answer would have been Albert Bierstadt, an artist schooled in the tradition of nature romanticism. Bierstadt was a painter of extraordinary skill and powerful imagination and his most stimulating experience had been with an exploratory expedition to the Rocky Mountains. Thus he was equipped to satisfy the yearnings of his contemporaries, to idealize the emergence of the nation in terms of nature. For them, Bierstadt was able to identify the tremendous landscapes of the far west with the romantic ideal of the sublime. Bierstadt's panoramic art, which brought the development of American landscape painting to a climax in the nineteenth century, satisfied a natural pride in the American accomplishment of becoming a truly continental nation, and at the same time, nourished a romantic ideal—"purple mountain majesties above the fruited plain." Hence the acclaim accorded Bierstadt a century ago.

Who could have imagined that one hundred years would bring such a revolutionary change in American life. And who could have imagined that the realist tradition would produce an artist as different from Bierstadt in style and outlook as Andrew Wyeth. Yet with both artists we find an unmistakable similarity in public response. Wyeth's draftsmanship and celebrated brush technique, and his gift for penetrating observation—not to mention his rural upbringing—have provided him with the experience and the mastery to forge his own expression and satisfy the yearnings of another age as no other living American artist has done.

The American preoccupation with territorial bigness that existed in Bierstadt's time vanished long ago. Bigness is taken for granted along with the duties and responsibilities that accompany it. As for the sublime, in a post-romantic age, we shy away from the word in any context. What we yearn for are those values that refute our materialism, oppose the encroachment of technological expansion and reject the madness of modern urban life. The art of Andrew Wyeth abounds in emblems which support these values, emblems that stir the heart of a tortured and disillusioned age. Simple pleasures, country people, solitude, the unexpected beauty of the commonplace, nature serene and inviolate, the quietude of the country — this is the repertory of Andrew Wyeth which evokes an anti-materialist image of America and offers panacea to our spiritual blight. Yet the same repertory if rendered by an artist of objective outlook, no matter how dazzling his technique, would not evoke the same response. Our generation in the tight embrace of technology yearns for the subjective. Andrew Wyeth conveys his message with a personal accent which gives an alluring privacy to his art, a quality as rare as it is prized in our over-public age.

The life and landscape of New England has nourished the artist's imagination for a long time now. Half of Andrew Wyeth's life is spent in Maine and half his art is devoted to it. Thus he joins a long line of New England painters which commenced in the early nineteenth century and embraces Fitz Hugh Lane, Winslow Homer, Childe Hassam, Maurice Prendergast, Marsden Hartley and John Marin, to mention a few. His name adds luster to an illustrious list.

While Andrew Wyeth's art has been seen at the William A. Farnsworth Library and Art Museum in Rockland, Maine, at the Massachusetts Institute of Technology where a selection of watercolors was mounted in 1960, and most importantly in a large show of his drawings and works in dry brush at the Fogg Art Museum in Cambridge in 1963, Andrew Wyeth has never had a comprehensive exhibition in New England. The occasion of the Museum's Centennial Year provides an especially appropriate moment to honor a distinguished continuity of this country's painters by holding an exhibition of one of its number, Andrew Wyeth, America's favorite artist, an artist New England can proudly claim.

The Officers and Trustees of the Museum of Fine Arts extend their special thanks to all those who have made the exhibition possible, and express their deep gratitude to the legion of individuals and institutions who have, with generosity and forbearance, made loans to this Centennial exhibition. A list of the lenders appears elsewhere.

The exhibition could not have taken place without the ready and patient assistance of both

Mr. and Mrs. Wyeth and E. Coe Kerr, the artist's dealer; nor without the effective collaboration of Frederick A. Sweet, Curator Emeritus of American Painting and Sculpture, The Art Institute of Chicago, who devoted himself to organizing and assembling the full range of Wyeth's work that is presented here.

Perry T. Rathbone, *Director*
Museum of Fine Arts, Boston

Lenders

ANDREW WYETH

I

Poets, painters, and musicians sometimes choose to live, and strictly operate, within a very special world defined by very special boundaries self-imposed. They do not set out to discover these worlds; they appear to be born within them. As they mature and develop, the shape and character of their environment, accepted or adapted, increasingly appear to strengthen and sustain them technically as well as philosophically. When we read, inspect, or listen to their work we enter into their domain far more than they do into ours. This, it seems to me, is always so. A reader unprepared for unicorns and gothic overtones will never cross the Danish doorsill of an Isak Dinesen to be enchanted. The cosmic quality of Robert Frost is locked up north of Boston. If you cannot reach his taproots, you will never sense his Emersonian power.

It is only the painter of course who makes his local habitation visible and gives it its true name. We see exactly where he lives and works and what, both animate and otherwise, inspires him. Even very different artists like Feininger or Klee or Joan Miró define in their own way imagination's other place. As Melville says, ''It is not down in any map: true places never are.''

Most people who know anything at all about the work of Andrew Wyeth are well aware of his private world. And not of his *one* world; of his two. These worlds, these places, *are* on any map of the eastern seaboard: Chadds Ford, Pennsylvania, where he was born, where he and his wife Betsy live quite simply, and Cushing, Maine, where he spends long summers. *Christina's World*, perhaps his most famous painting, is perfectly named since Christina's boundaries fall within his own in what some people think of as the northeast corner. Indeed his temperas, watercolors, dry-brush and pencil drawings are in many instances but an optical extension of her own so tragically restricted vision.

An extension, because Wyeth's symbols are almost all contained within his Pennsylvania and Maine anchorage: within essentially farm buildings, within the homely, simple landscape of the Brandywine Valley or an unspoiled slice of the Atlantic littoral. Even Thomas Eakins (1844–1916) — a Philadelphian unappreciated in his time, whom Wyeth much admires — had foreign influence, however native and however insular his work appears to be. "Eakins had a great humility," says Wyeth, who has more than enough of it himself to give his judgment value. "He went to the bottom of everything he did."

But Andrew Wyeth, fevered by the instant need of things, digs deeper into the intimate recesses of his private world even as Thoreau, the Delphic Yankee, dug deeply into Walden. We know that Thoreau's real companions were flora and fauna; Wyeth's are local friends and neighbors. Wyeth has *always* been the native son: unhappy traveler away from home, but tireless and uplifted walker on familiar ground, excited by the cleavages of sun and shadow, by implements, by weather, phrenology, a strand of wire, by surface textures — "I love white things. Oh, I love white." And who would doubt his love of doors and windows, of sudden contrasts between half in, half out? Doors and windows are a most important function of his imagination. The countryman knows this; the "Man from Maine" knows it; the city-blinded critic never. Wyeth could not say with one of E. M. Forster's characters: "How wonderful it must feel to belong to a city." Only a lover of a country winter can be a lover of the spring.

II

Youngest of five children, Andrew was lucky to have his father for a teacher. Born in Needham, Massachusetts, Newell Convers Wyeth, himself a pupil of Howard Pyle, was a muralist and delightful illustrator of a score of children's classics. I remember N. C. Wyeth most for robust color and for costumes clean of that cloud-castle romance as in Maxfield Parrish—another pupil of Howard Pyle. Somewhere along the line young Andrew learned at Chadds Ford what Degas in Paris—he died the year Wyeth was born—taught Mary Cassatt: *avoid sentimentality*. Starkness never tolerates the sentimental anyway.

I did not see his first one-man show at the William Macbeth Gallery, New York, in 1937 when the painter was twenty years old. I did see his 1938 show at the Doll and Richards Gallery in Boston. It was the sweep and freedom of those early watercolors—mostly Maine, it seems to me now—that bowled me over. I was looking into a brand-new world. Far from touching sentiment, the cold kelp-feeling of a down east wind kept blowing on me.

That very early wind could tell me: Rain, fire, smoke, suspended surf, flying birds, "the violent flamenco" of a hawk in flight, vehicles or animals in motion are not in the Wyeth lexicon. Even the boy running headlong at the bottom of the field—*Winter 1946*—and the same boy (too studied for my taste) on a bicycle—*Young America*—are caught as by a stroboscope. Likewise, so is *Soaring*, one of the several Wyeths that suggest the camera's influence, as in Eakins—but in the viewpoint only. The passing of time has only strengthened the painter's cryogenic approach.

Wyeth's passionate love of fallen snow—not falling snow—and of its zebra patterns, as he puts it, on a melting field; his fondness for bare textured surfaces, clean tabletops and windowpanes, all contribute to insulate him from the field of physical action. Even the powered dory in *The Wake*—and one may wonder if the froth *would* hang unbroken simultaneously around the circle's lip — even that dory with her prow far out of water and with more in the stern than meets the eye, seems without visible motion despite the visible thread-like wake. There is no bone in her teeth. With a fishing boat there would be. This is a physical demonstration: the right thing, right place, right moment.

Indeed, the casual viewer will observe, frame after frame, the way in which the brush is quicker than the eye. The crow is dead, the deer is dead, fields are deserted, plate and knife and cup and saucer spotless, shoes empty, a not too shapeless coat abandoned for the moment; a chimney is broken, ceilings are cracked, baskets and buckets battered; no oarlocks, oars, or water for some boats; antlers bare, seed corn dry, scissors open; the cistern closed. From the crescent beach the heron has flown, tools against a stump lean idle; apples lie frosted and cidery, the church bell mouth is mute; the logger's peavey poises upright on a log; one buttonwood, tremendous, rots at the root. Dogs, horse, and cows all stand implacable; a marsh hawk showing his fawn-colored vest and Dempsey shoulders sits on a post almost out of the picture to which he gives the title.

I am not wishing it otherwise, for all this has a bearing on the portrait-studies in particular. What is happening can best be described, I think, by reference to Scott Buchanan's brilliant modern essay, *Poetry and Mathematics*. Consider the Wyeth portraits by analogy. The subject — the solitary figure — represents a *cardinal* number. On the other hand the few enormously clear, familiar, and faultlessly placed objects — Wyeth calls them props — scissors, empty shoes, the blowing curtain in the *Chambered Nautilus*, the one-dimension decoy behind the three-dimension basket of apples (see p. 151) — represent *ordinal* numbers. The secret of clarity in prose is keeping the *ordinal* level. Santayana, as Buchanan says, moves elaborately among cardinal ideas. E. B. White, to me, moves at the ordinal level, as in his memorable essay in *One Man's Meat*, demolishing without a trace of vitriol the forgotten Townsend Plan. Mr. Townsend himself, in Mr. White's subsuming prose, comes just as vividly alive as Mr. Wyeth's figure called *The Swinger*. This is the end for which the poet does not always strive, but should. The cardinal figure of the poem supported by, and not submerged by, ordinals.

Looking back on the time when I first saw Andrew Wyeth's early watercolors and portraits and began to urge my friends to buy him, I think today it was a certain freedom and contagious quality of solitude and self-sufficiency I felt in his cool palette that had much earlier reached me in the tonal palette of the symphonies of Sibelius. One needs no title to recognize on page 163 the features of a Finn.

Once more I sense the tremendous compression of power and suggestion of intrinsic will which led my old friend and teacher, Paul J. Sachs of Harvard, to say of Wyeth's *Becky King*: "A penetrating observer who captures moods, gives proof in *Becky King*, as in all of his portraits, of the gulf that separates such a drawing, produced by a sensitive artist, from even the best photograph." There is no gulf between the beholder and this Finn or almost any Wyeth portrait. Show me the man who cares for trees—the rooted arch and muscled instep of the beech, the glove-grey texture of its bark; or for the dark, deep-shifting color values in massed pine or spruce—and I will gladly look into his mind and attitude toward art and toward the people who sit for him.

III

Some twenty years ago I wrote and published a series of quatrains called *Thirteen American Watercolors*, an introspective spectrum analysis which began with Winslow Homer and ended with Andrew Wyeth. This is the Wyeth quatrain. It is based on his Doll and Richards one-man watercolor show held in Boston in 1940:

Let fog burn off or shroud his coast of Maine:
No palette quite so cool, no stroke so sure.
Draftsman, great dramatist in iodine, and fain
To yield such simple things such strange allure.

I know now how Wyeth feels about watercolor which, in the right hands, puts the painter above the lyric poet. "A wonderful medium," says Mr. Wyeth. "You come on something in nature, you're excited, and you can let it out before you begin to think." Poetry, alas, is not always so instant.

Frosted Apples (p. 39) is a fine and later example of what I meant and mean by that quatrain. Which comes first, the gunny sack or tree? In area, the ordinal tree; in importance, the cardinal sack. At least two American poets have dealt with tipsy cows at random on the munch among some windfall apples. But the poetry of a half-filled burlap is a different matter. I once lugged enough of them in Oregon to know their feel, acridic smell, loose-woven texture. I get it here all over again. This is the communication that one looks for in the Wyeth drawing of a honeycomb or of a pair of shoes: something to be touched, something to be picked up, examined.

composed her there: two boxes, head, the wild flower cluster—possibly meadowsweet—devise the cross, bowlike as in the Archer.

Very little of the land- and town- or seascapes in the work of any artist is presented from a physical viewpoint inaccessible to him who cares to visit and inspect the original field, mountain, river, sand dune, village, avenue, façade, cathedral, tavern, silo, racetrack, quarry, ruin, forest, goldmine, or whatever. Anyone with cash and inclination can find, or nearly find, the spots where Monet stood; where Zorn would quickly swish his finished watercolor through the local horse trough just to soften up hard edges; or where Turner burned his latest sunset, Lear unpacked his wandering easel, or where Bierstadt looked upon the colors of the canyon. Or, if the spot evades the searcher simply for the lack of documented clues, at least he can say to himself, ''Well, I have seen things from this angle, in this light, and so on. And could I paint, this is *exactly* how I would or would not do the job.''

Now the least suggestive aspect of the present vision of pure Euclid in free space (p. 161) is that we climb a ladder, scale a slippery shingle roof, and shiver in the wind for no more reason than to check on how the painter set things up. We take his word, his concept, and his brush for answer. Perhaps because I have shingled part (the worst part) of a roof myself, I am identified, and quite familiar with this view. A Meryon or some daft young romantic would have flecked the sky with birds. One swallow surely brings this roof alive. And do not miss the other wings in flight—wings of his mate, no doubt— in silhouette against the conifers.

IV

Late afternoon, the way the sun is, on the idle hill of summer. (See p. 153.) Not as Housman knew it, but pure Wyeth, State of Maine: some daisy stars, ferns, goldenrod, dehiscent milkweed not yet loosed on the wind, one spiky tufted spruce just like the queer Australian tree down under, called the blackboy. The artist's wife asleep, the dog asleep; binoculars now emptied of their birds; the sun across the box of berries. I cannot look at this painting without saying to myself one stanza of Dr. Holmes's summer hymn called *Aestivation*, the lazy Latin current flowing through it:

How dulce to vive occult from mortal eyes,
Dorm on the herb with none to supervise,
Carp the suave berries from the crescent vine,
And bibe the flow from longicaudate kine!

When I was young and climbing Mt. Chocorua in New Hampshire, I stopped one day in running down the long and easy Hammond Trail to watch an older man: a meteorologist still closing in on the sky, but up there simply picking blueberries. You could tell from his sunburnt face and academic unconcern that there was more serenity in his head than berries in his pail.

Part of the business of art, as Santayana says of music, is to remind us. If a picture doesn't remind me of something in my life that I've forgotten, I am not involved. Small as they are, two boxes of berries (see p. 195), one brimful of pure cerulean, one half full of sun and shadow, are the symbols of that other deep-down shadow-world which we call sleep; the world whose rare and waking counterpart is total peace. Quite suddenly Chocorua, blueberries, and the weathervane on holiday come back to me. His sky is in it too; for the sleeper lies like a human constellation in the flowered field. The artist has

V

The first Andrew Wyeth that Robert Frost ever saw was *Turkey Pond*: a huge tempera in which a tall man is striding away from us from the bottom of the frame up through a wide and unmown field toward the high-horizon gleam of water and a thick green mass of needles: a very strong and striking composition. Just why it fascinated Frost I do not know, though I can guess. For me it is Orion by daylight, and I say:

> *In loneliness of flesh and blood and bone,*
> *Who walks as steadfast, and who walks alone?*

The other Wyeth work for which Frost cared (apart from a watercolor given him at Amherst on his eightieth birthday) is the widely reproduced tempera, *Wind from the Sea*. Frost never lived in Maine, but one of the old houses he acquired in the thirties way up the Connecticut River had the flavor and the age of this one. How the blowing curtains, the smell and taste of the sea, and the technical perfection of scrim or muslin transparency stick in the memory! There is more motion and buoyancy in this than in anything else the artist has done. He was thirty when he painted it; Frost was nearing seventy when he saw it first, and already beginning to get away from what in its simplicity had nourished him so long.

At the Amherst dinner (large attendance) on 26 March 1954, Robert's friend, Hyde Cox, made the presentation of a Wyeth watercolor (barn and open door, as I recall it). Said Mr. Cox in part: "We know that you share our high opinion of the work of Andrew Wyeth. . . . Moreover, the world Mr. Wyeth has created in his art seems to many people to have underlying affinity with the world of Robert Frost. I am not alone in feeling that a sympathy exists between these two unique and different worlds. . . . Andy Wyeth, himself, joins in the gift."

VI

There can be no doubt that Andrew Wyeth today is known to millions of people who could not name ten other American painters of any period. The fact that his reproductions sell by the thousands in the vast network of superstores across the continent, and that *Christina's World* confronts you as you buy a vacuum cleaner or a set of dishes should be evidence enough. How come, we ask ourselves, that at a time when cars and radios, TV's, bullhorns, hotrods, public-address systems, elevator music, outboards, and even snowmobiles in the country have taken over — how come we should see the wholesale purchase of a powerful silence? For silence — and silence absolute — is one of the strongest elements in Andrew Wyeth's work. Are people hungry for silence? I doubt that any city or Woodstock population is. Few of the young today can bear to be alone. The portable disk jockey in the pocket or under the arm on every sidewalk is just as anti-silence as the owner is likely anti-Dean, anti-family, or anti-Establishment. What I do not know is whether the young *buy* Wyeth. But he paints the silent minority.

One thing quite important which emerged from that first long and unselfconscious interview with Richard Meryman in 1960 was the word about Wyeth's love of costume. This explains his excitement in painting an old coat, his emphasis on curious boots — symbol of Death in one case; the reefer overcoat in *Buzzard's Glory*, his wife's very different coats in *French Twist* and in *Outpost*, the World War I uniform of *The Patriot*, the warmth of that (for Wyeth) highly-colored patchwork quilt in *Garrett Room*. Perhaps this is Emersonian compensation: first, the stark reality of nature, the stark reality of a sitter's features, the sitter's chair, the cold clean swept-up state of almost every room — that dilapidated sense of dignity; but dignity nevertheless. The freedom of the sketches is the burden of the balance.

VII

A lifelong habit of making mental notes of any work of art that has moved me often spills the notes into a journal. Under "W" for Wyeth are these entries:

Journal Entry: Wyeth uses water primarily as very small areas or surfaces incidental to his landscape. In *Weatherside* (p. 207) it is water in a pail; in *Hoffman's Slough* (p. 60) an integral part of the composition, but still minor; in *Wind from the Sea*, a suggestion: small in area, large in intent. In *River Cove* (p. 149) the sea has obviously moved in almost by stealth. Here it (the water) functions just to show the fearful narrow margin between life and death; life re-awakening under water, life extinct above high watermark. The sand looks like Texas limestone, which it isn't: all one mastermix of empty shells, razor-clam shells, all the sea's grafitti; three tracks of the great blue heron who was interrupted clearly visible. And dipping deep into that saline clarity, from the top of *River Cove*, reflection of the ancient life of evergreen.

Journal Entry: In his washes and preliminary sketches, Wyeth always seems to reach for the top of the paper. How many of his pictures are especially rewarding *just* at the top: the blind with cracks in it in *Wind from the Sea*, dry snow blowing off the roof in *Outpost*, suspension of the swing in *The Swinger*, so that the chains form a frame for the valley "maned with mist."

Journal Entry: "Maned with mist" is from *The Hill of Summer* by J. A. Baker, a young English naturalist with incredible powers of observation, persuasion, and a highly polished ordinal style. Nothing in nature is "dated" in man's temporal sense. What of Wyeth's natural subject matter? "Place is change," says Baker. "It is motion killed by the mind."

And *Blue Dump*, miraculous to me not least for that intoxicating purity of day which foggy Maine can suddenly produce. The river of stone outcrop so ingeniously aslant; the back of the driver's seat aimed right at that wide openness beyond. What light-and-shadow detail on the dump cart's panel behind the chain! Poets also find immediacy in simple unexpected things. This is William Carlos Williams on *The Red Wheelbarrow*:

so much depends
upon

a red wheel
barrow

glazed with rain
water

beside the white
chickens

Journal Entry: Without a grain of sentiment, and unlike Blake's small figure on the ladder to the moon: "I want, I want!", Wyeth tells us of his infinite own patience. His costumes and his masks at Halloween give him, for a moment, he has told us, anonymity: he just isn't there. If he never gets in the way of his work, his pictures never get in the way of our response. His black and outcast crows (see p. 73), which is Archibald MacLeish's phrase, are my crows too. I like them all the better because they are close to the ground, unromantic and businesslike: crows of my ancestral Lancaster County, Pennsylvania. I look, and hear them as I said once,

. . . . in the longbow of the year,
When the dead chestnut breaks upon the hill,

And the dark woods come darker still,
Because the light is younger where it shows
The clearest meadow and the blackest crows.

Journal Entry: Remembering that Wyeth's painter father was his teacher, reminds me that Harvey Cushing, the neurosurgeon, said: "It is a poor teacher whose student does not surpass him."

Journal Entry: A Wyeth critic I once read suggested, if I remember, that a cup and saucer, plate and a lonely knife on the table in *Groundhog Day* (see p. 35) meant that some loutish person would soon be eating there. How ignorant some city people are of the quality, wit and homely grace of the true countryman, farmer, maple-sugar man, the dairyman! A friend once told me of a farmer in New Hampshire inquiring about an octogenarian: "Does he still have all his facilities?" Another saying of his neighbor: "The wild pastures were her nursery." These are "louts"?

Journal Entry: So many Wyeth characters seem lost in thought; some of them full turned or partially turned away from the beholder. It is not alone these people, but the windows, and half-open doors that awaken what is in this couplet from *Ars poetica*:

For all the history of grief
An empty doorway and a maple leaf.

Journal Entry: We know a lot more today of work method than is in the Wyeth legend. The painter's incredible patience is something that one cannot acquire. Ralph Cline, of *The Patriot,* speaks of this. "Andy loses track of time, and if I'd been posing for some old crank, probably afore he got half done I might of broke the easel over his head. But if Andy wanted to work a little later, it was all right with me."

Journal Entry: The remarkable whitewashing of the light in *Cooling Shed* (see p. 75). How could this be old hat in the time of Rembrandt, in Wyeth's time, or after 1984 if we should reach it?

Journal Entry: As to Wyeth's concern with costume: consider Eakins' portrait of Frank Hamilton Cushing in a frontier trapper's outfit. The costume may become cardinal and the poser ordinal. Not so in Wyeth's *The Patriot* or *The Finn*; but at least partially so in *Maga's Daughter*.

Journal Entry: In *Nicholas*, the coat—cardinal above the ordinal—wins out.

Journal Entry: (Returning to *Frosted Apples*.) Apple wood on the fire is the only wood I know that burns, like a fine cigar, to a pure white ash. In its old age in the orchard (as in the watercolor) it is the most crusty, lichenous, and pocked of all our trees; the next most twisty to the cypress and the cedar. It is pruned for right angles. Comfort me with apples? How comfortable the sack!

Journal Entry: To that "powerful silence" one must add "enormous stillness."

Journal Entry: A brooding silence hangs over the Wyeth landscapes; it is not confined to a room. By night, one would expect at most the soundless distant flicker of heat lightning—never the Burchfield revelation: fearful trees and sparky flowers out of a sylvan Leyden jar.

Journal Entry: Blue, so sparsely used by Wyeth—no real blue skies—is more telling when it comes: perhaps a blue chair out in the sun. Winslow Homer, whom Wyeth also admires and whose influence was evident a little in the early watercolors, was likewise sparing, and thereby the more emphatic with his use of blue, especially in accents.

Journal Entry: I hate poetry with music. Poems should not be illustrated.

And it is probably best with painting to go off into a corner and have your say: not right up against what is saying something all by itself. As for criticism, in art or anything else, it dies for me when the peck order enters into it. It should take off for free.

Journal Entry: "The world about us would be desolate except for the world within us. There is the same interchange between these two worlds that there is between one art and another, migratory passings to and fro, quickenings, Promethean liberations and discoveries." — Wallace Stevens: *The Relations between Poetry and Painting*.

Journal Entry: But in that simple matter of reminding, a painting will recall a line of verse much faster than the other way around. The thought of Wyeth's patience, and his concern with nature brings up two lines from Mark Van Doren:

A little water will put out the fire.
But wait. A little wood will keep it breathing.

Journal Entry: I come again and again to the tentative washes. They rightly omit so much.

VIII

All these are the random notes of one who thinks he understands one artist's commitment to his art. Ability, no matter where it stands on the scoreboard of genius, is a great factor. Great also are humility and honesty. Hokusai: "An old man mad about drawing." Andrew Wyeth: A fairly young man still; still mad about drawing. "I feel very much a part of today," he told Selden Rodman. "The other day I took the boys to the airport. I took my sketchbook too. I sat there with the planes flying around us, drawing like crazy. I was perfectly at home and perfectly happy. I'd like to do a painting of the vapor trails of jets."

As Robert Frost said in one final and finial monosyllabic line, all ordinals rising to the cardinal thought:

We love the things we love for what they are.

David McCord

PENNSYLVANIA

27   *MONDAY MORNING. Tempera, 1955, 12 x 16½ in.*
Collection of Mr. and Mrs. John Hay Whitney, New York
This really should be titled "Tuesday Morning" because the artist's wife had washed on
Monday and left the clothes on the line overnight. In the morning her washbasket was
drifted with snow that had fallen during the night.

29

31 *ALAN. Dry brush, 1955, 5 x 5 in.*
Lent by Mrs. Andrew Wyeth
This is not Allan Lynch. He had moved away and a tall lanky boy had taken his place,
Alan Messersmith. He wandered freely in and out of the Wyeths' house. Although
older, he enjoyed the company of the Wyeth boys. His sled was always the fastest,
his stories the best. This drawing was done in preparation for "Roasted Chestnuts."

37 *OIL DRUM. Watercolor, 1957, 13¾ x 21¾ in.*
   Lent by Henry A. Loeb, New York
*Winter at the Kuerners'. Everything is taken care of because they have worked hard to
earn it. You will never see a piece of farm machinery left out in the weather. Even an
oil drum is carefully covered with canvas to keep it from rusting.*

43   *GROUNDHOG DAY. Tempera, 1959, 31 x 31¼ in.*
   Lent by the Philadelphia Museum of Art
We are inside the Kuerners' warm kitchen looking out the window at the log that appears
in "First Snow." Karl's place has been set at the kitchen table for the noonday meal. When
he comes in from the barn he will wash his hearty meal down not only with coffee but
with beer kept on draught in the cold entryway.

60 *CHESTER COUNTY. Watercolor, 1962, 22½ x 30¾ in.*
Lent by Mr. and Mrs. William S. Cook, Tenants Harbor, Maine
There was about Tom Clark just a suggestion of a mysterious heritage. His features were sharp and his eyes a disarming blue. As he sat in his morris chair, posing, the stove pipe became a crown that he wore with great dignity, and the blue of his garret ceiling, royal.

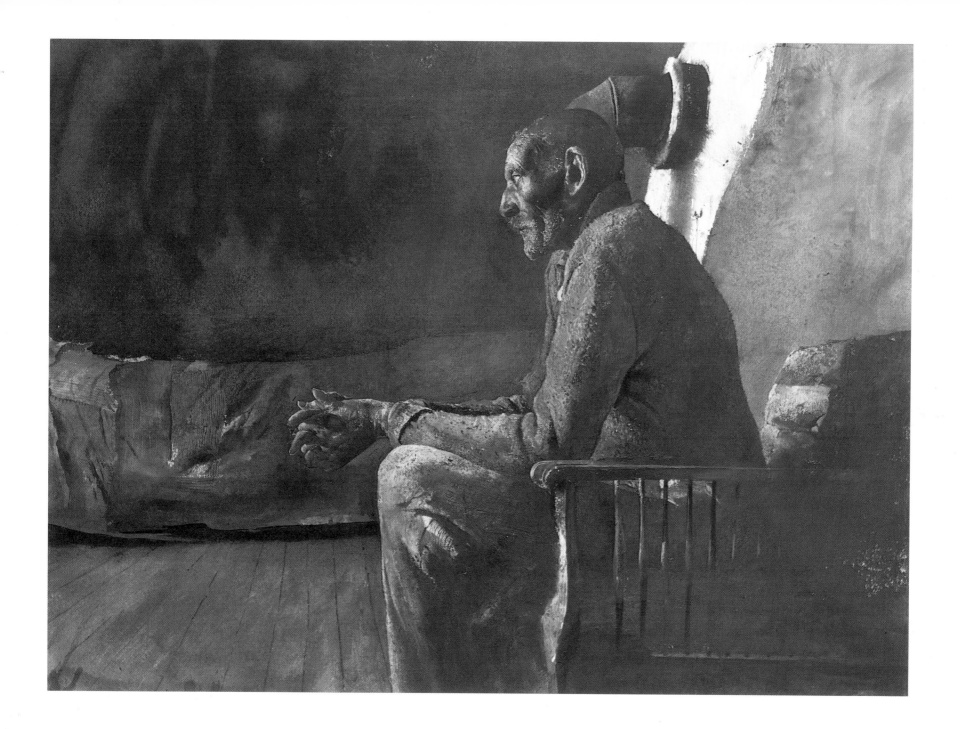

79 FROSTED APPLES. *Watercolor, 1967, 20 x 28 in.*
    Lent anonymously
This bag, half full of apples, could have been full of anything. Maybe left by a tramp. The
important object in this picture is that bag and its hidden contents. Great care has been
taken in the texture of the burlap and the bulging shapes. The reason could go as far back
as reaching for a stocking hung on a bedpost in the dark of early Christmas morning.

80   *FRENCH TWIST. Dry brush, 1967, 22½ x 28½ in.*
       Lent by Mrs. Andrew Wyeth
*Betsy is seated at the head of a long table in their house. The flair of her coat and the grip
of her hands on the table give the figure a feeling of immediate action. Any moment she
will stand up and stride away. Hanging from a hook over the massive fireplace opening
is a bell that she might reach for and start ringing.*

82 *OUTPOST. Tempera, 1968, 23½ x 23¼ in.*
Lent by Mrs. Andrew Wyeth
You are under the carriage shed at the mill looking out at Betsy in the same broad-brim-
med hat she wore in "The Country." The construction of the shed with the supporting
downposts shows in "Marsh Hawk." Behind her is the granary. It is a snowy, blowy day.
She could be a sentry standing at any winter outpost, on any frontier.

84 *SLIGHT BREEZE. Tempera, 1968, 24½ x 32½ in.*
Lent by Mrs. James Wyeth, Chadds Ford

In the evening you can see the lights of the Woodward barn from Brinton's Mill. The farm lies up river from the mill. One spring morning Wyeth rowed up, tied his boat to a limb, and walked across the tilled fields to the house. There around the corner of the building he came upon this drying yard, the farm bell freshly painted and a few things on the clothesline blowing in the slight breeze.

87 *BUZZARD'S GLORY. Tempera, 1968, 18 x 23⅜ in.*
        Lent by Mr. and Mrs. Joseph E. Levine, New York
Johnny Lynch strongly resembles his first cousin, Allan. He even walked around town
wearing an army coat, the collar turned up the same way Allan would turn his. That
mane of black hair and the tilt of his eyes — all Lynch. Several families of Lynches once
lived along a stretch of road in Chadds Ford known as Buzzard's Glory. The story goes
that one of them would shoot buzzards circling over the marsh, roast them, and serve
buzzard for Sunday dinner.

99 *AFTERNOON FLIGHT. Dry brush, 1970, 22⅜ x 28⅜ in.*
   Lent by the artist

*The artist came upon Jimmy Lynch in the crook of an apple tree in the orchard watching
a squirrel run across the field to the woods. Or was he watching a jet streak across the
horizon, or a buzzard high overhead? Jimmy has tried a little of everything — quarreling
with the changes he cannot control, yearning for a different life, but not wanting to be
tied down to any one thing.*

100   *LYNCH. Dry brush, 1970, 21 x 29 in.*
     Lent by the artist
Jimmy is a defiant youth. He's been blamed for a lot of things he did not do, and he has done a lot of things he has taken the blame for. His own father he knew only slightly. His stepfather died when he was in his early teens. Jimmy trusts his dogs and very few people. One of them is Andrew Wyeth.

1   WINTER FIELDS. *Tempera, 1942, 17¼ x 41 in.*
   Lent by Mr. and Mrs. Benno C. Schmidt, New York
*If you should walk across the country directly in back of N. C. Wyeth's studio you would
cross this field. On just such a walk, the artist found a dead crow lying frozen on the
ground. He carried it back to his studio and made two careful, detailed drawings with ink
and watercolor. Then he returned to the field and made a dry brush drawing of the landscape from life. By combining the crow drawings with the landscape study, "Winter
Fields" was completed.*

2 *SPRING BEAUTY. Dry brush, 1943, 20 x 30 in.*
   The F. M. Hall Collection, University of Nebraska, Lincoln, Nebraska
A favorite walk leads from N. C. Wyeth's studio, through the woods, out onto open fields,
passing Adam Johnson's farm, down the hill to Mother Archie's Church and ending at
Karl Kuerner's. If something on the way catches the artist's eye, he stops to make a
watercolor or a drawing. One early spring day he found the first spring beauty of the
season blooming at the base of a giant beech tree.

3 *MOTHER ARCHIE'S CHURCH. Tempera, 1945, 25 x 48 in.*
   Lent by the Addison Gallery of American Art, Phillips Academy, Andover, Massachusetts

Just up the road from the Kuerner farm, within sight of Adam Johnson's, are the ruins of this octagonal church. Just the walls are left standing today. Once the building had been a school, later a Negro church. After Mother Archie, the minister, died, fewer services were held. When Wyeth painted this tempera, the pigeons were using the building as a roost.

4 WINTER 1946. *Tempera, 1946, 31⅜ x 48 in.*
   Lent anonymously

Directly across the road from Karl Kuerner's farm this hill rises. He owns it. Over the brow of the hill are the fields and woods that lead to the artist's studio. In 1946 a family by the name of Lynch were living in a house on the edge of the woods. This was a large family—nineteen children. You would meet them along the path in the woods or crossing the fields. One day the artist looked up to see Allan Lynch running down the hill towards him for no reason other than the joy of running.

5 *WINTER MORNING. Dry brush, 1946, 25 x 37½ in.*
   Lent anonymously
This is the side of Karl Kuerner's barn with his house beyond. Kuerners' hill of "Winter 1946" rises in front. Deer season never ends without Karl shooting his deer. German by birth and frugal by nature, every edible part of this deer will be carefully saved. At Christmas he will give his friend, the artist, a gift of venison.

6 *FOUR POSTER. Dry brush, 1946, 40 x 29½ in.*
Lent by Mrs. Roger Milliken, Spartanburg, South Carolina
If you approach the village of Chadds Ford from the east, you will
pass on your right Brandywine Battlefield Park which is main-
tained by the State of Pennsylvania. Within the park limits sits
the stone house, Lafayette's headquarters. This detailed drawing of
the ground floor bedroom was done long before the bitter court
battle that resulted in Lafayette's headquarters passing from pri-
vate ownership into state hands.

7 *ARTHUR CLEVELAND. Tempera, 1946, 42 x 30¾ in.*
Lent by The Wilmington Society of the Fine Arts, Delaware
The owner of Lafayette's headquarters stands in the bedroom.
A tall man with a booming, rich voice, the low ceilinged house
always seemed lower when he entered. Losing his ownership of
the house in the court battle broke his health, and he died before
the court order to move came into effect.

59

8 *HOFFMAN'S SLOUGH. Tempera, 1947, 30 x 55 in.*
    Lent by Mr. and Mrs. Charles Mayer, New York
The Brandywine River runs through the village of Chadds Ford. High on the west bank
you can look down onto the meandering course of the river, the water meadows with
marshes and sloughs, to the hills on the other side. On the side of the hill in Hoffman's
Slough sits the stone house of John Chads. Travelers fording the river at his property
soon called the crossing Chadds Ford.

9 *KARL. Tempera, 1948, 30⅝ x 23⅝ in.*
    Lent anonymously
A portrait of Karl Kuerner. He posed in a room on the third floor of his farmhouse.
Embedded in the plaster of the ceiling are iron hooks. From these hooks Karl hangs
links of sausages and the hams he cures. Most of Wyeth's portraits are painted where
the sitter lives. He feels if he removed a person from their everyday environment he
might lose a valuable sense of their surroundings, even though no objects appear in
the picture.

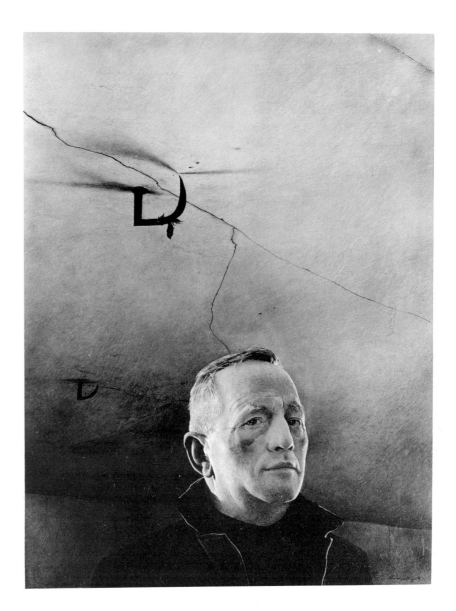

10 WINTER CORN. *Dry brush, 1948, 29 x 38 in.*
   Lent anonymously
Corn fields are crossed on the artist's walk from his studio up the hill to his father's
studio and beyond to Adam Johnson's, Archie's Church, and Kuerner's. Karl would
never leave a stalk standing in his fields but other farmers often do. "Winter Corn"
was done before the wild creatures of winter fed on the dried kernels.

11 *McVEY'S BARN. Tempera, 1948, 32½ x 48 in.*
Lent by the New Britain Museum of Art, Connecticut (Harriet Russell Stanley Fund)

The property next to the artist's studio was once owned by the farmer John McVey. He died and the farm was sold, but up in the loft of the unused barn McVey's sleigh was stored. After this picture was completed, the new owner lowered the sleigh down and had it upholstered in bright red velvet. When last seen it was sitting in a store window as a Christmas decoration.

12   *TILLIE TAGGERT. Watercolor, 1948, 23½ x 29¼ in.*
Museum of Fine Arts, Boston (Anonymous gift in memory of Nicholas Jarrot
Tiffany and Lt. George Shepley Tiffany)
This was the year Mr. Taggert died leaving a large family of children and their mother
unsupported. Mysteriously, one day the family simply vanished—less than a week after
Tillie posed in Archie's Church for this picture. A neighbor said: "The Amish came in
their black carriages, packed them all up and drove off."

13 *THE CLOISTERS. Tempera, 1949, 32 x 41 in.*
    Lent by The Art Institute of Chicago (Gift of Mrs. Joseph Regenstein)
*On the outer edge of the town of Ephrata, Pennsylvania, sits a cluster of stone and
frame buildings that were built by a religious group in the early 1700's and have become
known as The Cloisters. By the time Wyeth made his first visit, the sect had dwindled
down to one family. They took him through every building. In a room on the upper floor
of one he was struck by the sun slanting across the wall bringing out the gold of the mud
plaster. He had often noticed the same color on a chalk parrot he owned at home.*

14 *CHILDREN'S DOCTOR. Tempera, 1949, 26 x 25 in.*
   Lent by Margaret I. Handy, Chadds Ford
The artist's son Nicholas had been severely ill, and it was necessary for the doctor to drive out from her office for frequent house visits. On several occasions Dr. Margaret Handy would arrive at the house clearly showing the strain of a sleepless night — her car mud-spattered from country roads, but her attitude calm and her judgment keen. All was well while she was there, but then she would leave, often in the night, to visit another sick child.

15 *YOUNG AMERICA. Tempera, 1950, 32½ x 46 in.*
Lent by The Pennsylvania Academy of the Fine Arts, Philadelphia
Here is Allan Lynch four years after "Winter 1946." Someone had thrown a bicycle on
the dump. Allan retrieved it, painted it up, mounted an aerial with a foxtail on it, tied
streamers to the handlebars, and roamed the country roads with his prize—a counter-
part to the motorcycle-sports car youth of today. Most of his clothes were Army and
Navy store purchases which he wore with a swagger. Sixteen years later Allan took his
own life.

16 *NIGHT LAMP. Tempera, 1950, 14¼ x 20 in.*
  Lent by Mrs. Frank A. Elliott, Philadelphia
A lamp in the window of Mother Archie's Church. No one seemed to object when a newly-wed couple moved into the vacant building, put up temporary partitions to divide off the eight-sided room, and spent their first year of marriage under the shadow of Kuerner's hill.

17 *THE TRODDEN WEED. Tempera, 1951, 20 x 18¼ in.*
Lent by Mrs. Andrew Wyeth
The artist has said on more than one occasion, ''I'm really a swashbuckler at heart.''
Here are his feet tramping the fields near Karl Kuerner's—the familiar hill in the far
distance, black coat blowing in the winter wind. He considers this his only self-portrait.

18 *FARAWAY. Dry brush, 1952, 13½ x 21 in.*
   Lent by Mrs. Andrew Wyeth
Jamie, the artist's younger son, was five years old that spring. Ever since he could walk
he'd been with his father either in the studio or crossing fields. In the fall he would be
going to school. On a path above the studio this picture was done from life.

19 *TARPAULIN. Watercolor, 1953, 20 x 29 in.*
   Lent by Walter S. Carpenter, Jr., Wilmington, Delaware
*Adam Johnson has thrown a tarpaulin over his fence. Down the hill is Mother Archie's
Church. Not only the physical features of the people he paints interest Wyeth but also
the way they place objects on their land. The way Karl Kuerner hangs a dead deer from
his barn, the way Adam throws a tarpaulin over a fence.*

20 *THE CORNER. Dry brush, 1953, 13½ x 21½ in.*
  Lent by The Wilmington Society of the Fine Arts, Delaware
The tenants had moved from the frame house and the young couple had left Mother
Archie's Church. The property had been sold. The surrounding acreage was being
divided into house lots. Before anything happened to the actual buildings this intimate
dry brush was done. A year later, the house was torn down and the church nothing
but a shell.

21   *FLOCK OF CROWS. Dry brush, 1953, 9½ x 19 in.*
   Lent by Mrs. Andrew Wyeth
Beyond Archie's Church in "The Corner" you will see this slope. This drawing was done
as a preliminary study for the tempera "Snow Flurries" and shows an intimate detail of
a much larger whole. It is part of the Kuerner farm.

22 *SNOW FLURRIES. Tempera, 1953, 36 x 47 in.*
   Lent by Margaret I. Handy, Chadds Ford
This hill is in truth a hill of much smaller size. The road up it leads to Karl Kuerner's back fields. Combined in this picture are the open feeling of Karl's entire farm and the Pennsylvania hills of winter.

23 *COOLING SHED. Tempera, 1953, 24¾ x 12⅜ in.*
   Lent by Mrs. Frank A. Elliott, Philadelphia
It was spring. Before leaving for Maine the artist drove up the river valley to see his friend John Wylie and place his winter order for firewood. Wylie was away, but the door leading into his shed was open. Stepping inside Wyeth could see at the end of a long passageway Wylie's spring room bathed in light. There glistening in the sun were the pails and cans beside the trough.

24   KARL'S ROOM. *Watercolor, 1954, 21½ x 29¾ in.*
Lent by The Museum of Fine Arts, Houston, Texas (Gift of Mrs. W. S. Farish)
Immediately after World War I Karl Kuerner left Germany with all his belongings
packed in this trunk. He rented a farm at Chadds Ford and worked hard to buy it
eventually. Through the years he bought more land and became known as an expert
shot and much respected farmer. Here is a corner of his bedroom.

25 *WALTER SAMUEL CARPENTER III. Tempera, 1954, 34 x 41½ in. (framed)*
Lent by Mrs. W. S. Carpenter III, Greenville, Delaware
Knights and Robin Hood and dashing pirates have never quite left the artist's nature.
Here is a handsome friend who wears his Spanish bullfighter's jacket with a flair. A
trace of Spanish blood runs through Mr. Carpenter's veins, and this is how the artist
saw him one evening at dinner.

26 *CORNER OF THE WOODS. Tempera, 1954, 38½ x 30½ in.*
Lent anonymously

This corner beech tree marks the point where the back of the N. C. Wyeth property makes a turn. Several times as the artist's wife, Betsy, sat posing, deer came so close that the Wyeths could have reached out and touched them.

27 *MONDAY MORNING. Color plate, p. 29*

28 *NICHOLAS. Tempera, 1955, 32½ x 30¾ in.*
Lent by Mrs. Andrew Wyeth

When the artist's older son, Nicholas, would arrive home from school each day, the first thing he would do before even taking off his jacket would be to walk through the rooms to his father's studio. He would sit down and talk about his day. Usually his father would be interested, but one day he was so busy working at his easel that Nicholas stopped talking and just sat. When his father looked around to see if he was gone, this is what he saw.

29 *CIDER AND PORK. Watercolor, 1955, 21 x 28½ in.*
Lent by Amanda K. Berls, New York
Karl Kuerner's spring house is on the drive going in. The door is always unlocked. This is where he keeps his barrels of homemade cider to ferment slowly. A friend is welcome to draw off a cup. One day the door was opened and in the familiar darkness hung the side of a newly slaughtered pig.

30 *ALEXANDER CHANDLER. Dry brush, 1955, 21½ x 15 in.*
Collection of Mr. and Mrs. Robert Montgomery, New York
On the high ground above the village of Chadds Ford is another town, called Dilworthtown. The main highways have passed it by. In a cluster of buildings live several Negro families. This blind man sitting in the hot, noonday sun caught the artist's eye as he was driving by.

31 *ALAN. Color plate, p. 31*

32 *ROASTED CHESTNUTS. Tempera, 1956, 48 x 33 in.*
   Lent by Mr. and Mrs. Harry G. Haskell, Jr., Chadds Ford
Alan Messersmith was an organizer. One fall he went into the
business of selling chestnuts along the main highway, and he needed
help. The artist's sons were recruited along with other neighboring
boys. For hours they would stand by the road in the freezing cold
selling bags of hot chestnuts. Alan still outsold them all. His father, a
tinsmith by trade, had converted a large oil drum into a charcoal stove
and on the top a dish-like arrangement held the roasting chestnuts.
Soon the helpers lost interest, but Alan kept his post until snow.

33 *TOM CLARK. Watercolor, 1956, 10½ x 11 in.*
   Lent by Mrs. Andrew J. Sordoni, Jr., Forty Fort, Pennsylvania
Tom's brother had worked for the N. C. Wyeths for years. Only
occasionally would you catch a glimpse of Tom's tall figure walking
down the road with a cloth satchel on his way to the store. He lived
by the railroad tracks across the river from the village. One day
Wyeth stopped at his house and found him sleeping.

34 *GRANDDAUGHTER. Dry brush, 1956, 16½ x 23½ in.*
   Collection of Mr. and Mrs. Robert Montgomery, New York
Back in Dilworthtown Alexander Chandler dozes in the sun. His
granddaughter, Kathy Hunt, impatiently stands waiting for her
grandfather to give her a nickle to spend at the store.

35 ROPE AND CHAINS. *Pencil drawing, 1956, 16¾ x 22¾ in.*
Lent by Mrs. Andrew Wyeth
There is only one reason for this rope hanging from a limb at Karl Kuerner's.
It is used to hoist a slaughtered pig up to drain off the blood that will be carefully
collected for blood sausage. Although the rope appears as the smallest detail in
the tempera ''Brown Swiss,'' doing the drawing served its purpose by submerging
the artist in Karl Kuerner's surroundings.

36 BROWN SWISS. *Tempera, 1957, 30½ x 61 in.*
Lent by Mr. and Mrs. Alexander M. Laughlin, New York
One evening driving home Wyeth stopped his car and waited while Karl Kuerner
drove his herd of Brown Swiss cattle across the road to his barn. Sitting there he
was impressed by the reflection of Kuerner's house in his farm pond, banked by
brown hills, crisscrossed with cow paths.

37 OIL DRUM. *Color plate, p. 33*

38 *CITIZEN CLARK. Dry brush, 1957, 14⅜ x 22⅜ in.*
   Lent by Mr. and Mrs. Alexander M. Laughlin, New York
The artist has long been attracted to people who live out their lives at home. Tom Clark
had all the time in the world to pose—nothing hurried, nothing interrupted the easy flow
of his conversation as he sat in his kitchen. He even had decided he had paid taxes long
enough. "If they want to come and get me, they'll have to take me out piece by piece
through the keyhole."

39 *BRINTON'S MILL. Dry brush, 1957, 13¼ x 21½ in.*
Lent by the Wyeth Endowment for American Art: Boston Safe Deposit and Trust
Company, Trustee
Eventually this was to become the Wyeths' home. This mill lies a mile up the valley
from the village. N. C. Wyeth often brought his children here to swim below the dam.
His teacher, Howard Pyle, first took him there in 1903. Perhaps the imposing stone
façade of the mill reminded Pyle of the medieval fortresses of Europe that he so
frequently illustrated. This dry brush was done as a pre-study for ''Raccoon.''

40 *RACCOON. Tempera, 1958, 48 x 48 in. (framed)*
   Lent by Mr. and Mrs. Harry G. Haskell, Jr., Chadds Ford
*When the artist saw these dogs tied to the front entrance of the mill he wondered who
lived there. He soon found out that the owner seldom let them run—only for coon hunts.
Limited to their chained area, they had survived the heat of summer and the cold of
winter with quiet patience. Wyeth tried to purchase Jack, the hound in the foreground,
but the owner refused and shot him in a drunken rage.*

41 *THE MILL. Dry brush, 1958, 12 x 22¼ in.*
    Lent by Mrs. Andrew Wyeth
*After Brinton's Mill was purchased by the Wyeths and reconstruction begun, the artist
made this record of the mill, the granary, and the miller's house. The mill itself had
become a roost for pigeons and a flight can be seen in silhouette against the late afternoon sky.*

42 *FIRST SNOW. Dry brush, 1959, 13⅜ x 21¼ in.*
  Lent by The Wilmington Society of the Fine Arts, Delaware
*During the winter months Karl Kuerner and his son, always
known as Young Karl, spend much time splitting wood. A huge
tree trunk has been dragged by tractor near the house so that when
splitting begins the wood can be stacked in the nearby shed. When
this painting had been completed, ''Groundhog Day'' was begun.*

43 *GROUNDHOG DAY. Color plate, p. 35*

44 *FUNGUS. Watercolor, 1959, 29¾ x 21½ in.*
  Lent by Mr. and Mrs. J. Bruce Bredin, Greenville, Delaware
*Quite often the artist will turn from his involvement with people
and their houses and be totally alone in a field of corn, along a
river bank, or in the woods, which is where he found this fungus
living on a broken limb.*

91

45 *WINTER BEES. Dry brush, 1959, 21 x 27 in.*
   Lent by Mrs. Andrew Wyeth
*Close by the trees where he painted "Fungus," the artist discovered a beehive hanging
from the limb of a beech. First he made a careful pencil drawing, then started in with
watercolor. This was never completed because a raccoon tore the hive apart one night.*

46 *RACE GATE. Watercolor, 1959, 18½ x 25 in.*

     Lent by Mr. and Mrs. Leslie P. Ogden, Harrison, New York

To control the flow of water into Brinton's Mill, the head gates would be slid up and pins stuck through the holes in the shafts to keep the gates raised. For over ten years the gates had been closed; the water lay silent in the mill pond, the wood rotting in the dampness of a wet snow.

47 *MORNING SUN. Dry brush, 1959, 13½ x 21 in.*

    Lent by Mr. and Mrs. Mortimer Spiller, Buffalo, New York

Often a study, such as this one of Tom Clark caught in the morning sun, will end as that; but something here made the artist go further. He spent more and more time at Clark's house. And so in looking back you might say that "Morning Sun" was done in preparation for "That Gentleman."

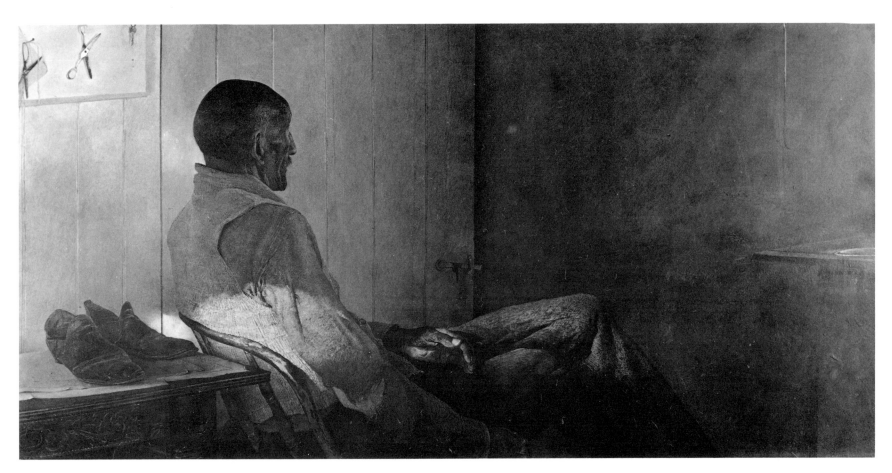

48   *THAT GENTLEMAN. Tempera, 1960, 23½ x 47¾ in.*
   Lent by the Dallas Museum of Fine Arts, Texas

*Tom Clark went about the business of living in a very orderly way. He would prepare
his vegetables with a deft grace, mend his clothes with care, lift the lid of a kettle seconds
before it would boil over, keep his wood stove just the right temperature, place his slip-
pers on a newspaper so as not to soil the table top. This tall, thin gentleman always re-
ferred to objects—whether a potato, an annoying fly buzzing overhead, or a car passing
by—as "that gentleman."*

49 *AFTER SHAVING. Watercolor, 1960, 20½ x 30 in.*
  Lent by Mrs. Colin Gardner, Middletown, Ohio
*During the warm months Tom Clark would draw a basin of water at the pump, carry it
out on the porch where a smoky mirror hung on the side of the house, and set about his
morning shave with a sharp-edged razor, expertly handled.*

50 *UP IN THE WOODS. Watercolor, 1960, 21½ x 29 in.*
  Lent by Amanda K. Berls, New York
*"Up in the woods" is a family expression. "I'll meet you up in the woods." "We will
have our Easter picnic up in the woods." "Let's take a walk up in the woods." The N. C.
Wyeth home overlooks Chadds Ford, which is in a valley. Higher still are the woods be-
hind it, and it is there that this watercolor was painted one snowy February day.*

51 *MAY DAY. Watercolor, 1960, 12½ x 29 in.*
Lent by Mrs. Andrew Wyeth
This frieze of spring beauties grew along the banks of Wyeth's raceway at Brinton's Mill.
When he brought the picture back home, he cut the top half off because he realized that
by showing the trees and sky above he was losing the freshness of new wild flowers
blooming amid the tangle of dank undergrowth.

52   *THE DAM. Watercolor, 1960, 10⅜ x 14½ in.*
     Lent by Mrs. Andrew Wyeth
This tiny picture was done very quickly while large, wet snowflakes fell on the lower dam at Brinton's Mill. The snow muffled the roar of the dam as the flakes fell and disappeared in the black water.

53 YOUNG BULL. *Dry brush, 1960, 19¾ x 41¼ in.*
    Lent by Mrs. Andrew Wyeth
A young Brown Swiss bull stands alongside the wall enclosing Karl Kuerner's barnyard.
Beyond the wall is the same hill Allan Lynch ran down in "Winter 1946." Out of sight
beyond the wall in front of the house is the farm pond of "Brown Swiss." A few of the
top limbs of the tree where the pigs hang can be seen over the top of the wall. The bull
was not always this patient. One day he gave a quick kick that sent Wyeth's palette fly-
ing, spattering color across the unfinished picture. A trace remains on the side of the bull.

54 *MILK CANS. Dry brush, 1961, 13¼ x 20¾ in.*
    Lent by Mrs. Andrew Wyeth
A long period of dry cold had settled in to stay. Coming across the field to Adam John-
son's farm, the artist found these two milk cans Adam had placed beside a pen. The flat,
bleached light of intense cold is everywhere. The drawing was never completed.

55 *TENANT FARMER. Tempera, 1961, 30½ x 40 in.*
Lent by The Wilmington Society of the Fine Arts, Delaware
Wyeth is not at all interested in eighteenth-century buildings be-
cause they are eighteenth-century. He may care what age has
done to the texture of a brick or stone or wood building, but in the
same way he would be interested in the bark of a tree. What led
to this tempera was the deer hanging from a graceful willow tree
while a dry snow blew off the roof and disappeared in the howling
wind. He did not know the tenants who occupied the house.

56 *BACK APARTMENT. Watercolor, 1961, 30¼ x 22 in.*
Lent by Mr. and Mrs. Donald S. Gilmore, Kalamazoo,
Michigan
Christian Sanderson, a bachelor, occupied three rooms in the back
part of this house. His rooms were choked with the accumulation
of a lifetime of collecting. No effort was made to keep order. This
haphazard patch of rotting tomatoes seemed like the contents of
Cris's house, spilling out onto the side yard.

57 *THE GRANARY. Watercolor, 1961, 13⅝ x 21⅝ in.*
  Lent by Mrs. Andrew Wyeth
This picture of the granary building at Brinton's Mill was completed with much the same
quick intensity used in painting "The Dam." The snow was wet and the mud-colored
stone buildings seemed to soak it up. By this time the artist was living in the granary
waiting for the miller's house, on the right, to be completed.

58 *BRITISH AT BRANDYWINE. Dry brush, 1962, 19½ x 25½ in.*
Lent by Mr. and Mrs. Walter J. Laird, Jr., Wilmington, Delaware
The granary at Brinton's Mill had once been a stable. The windows were high and small.
On the stone sill a few lead soldiers had been placed. Light fell on them just as it had on
September 11th, 1777, when the British army swarmed through the valley the day they
fought the Americans at the battle of the Brandywine.

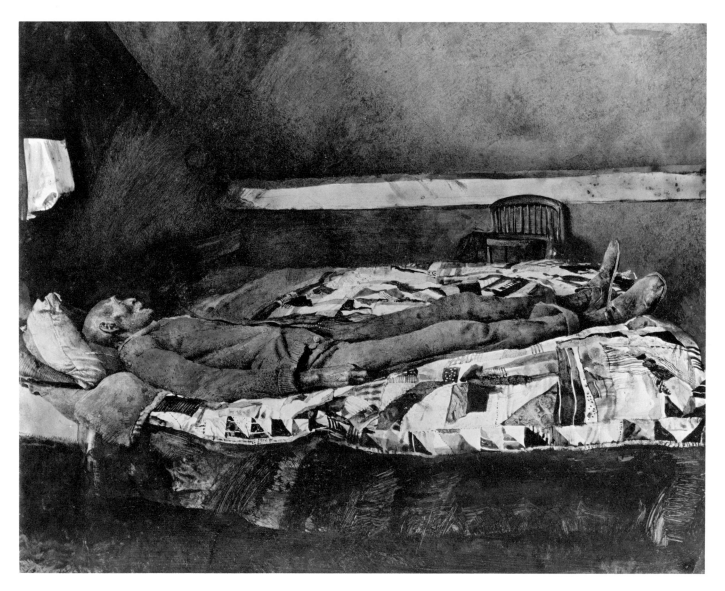

59 *GARRET ROOM. Dry brush, 1962, 17½ x 22½ in.*
      Lent by Mrs. Andrew Wyeth

Tom Clark, all six-feet-two of him, lies stretched out on his bed asleep. He was getting older and sleep came easily. He almost seems longer than life. In fact when he died a year later, his daughter looked at this picture, and, thinking aloud, reminded herself to call the funeral parlor to order a coffin two inches longer so that Tom could be buried with his shoes on.

60 *CHESTER COUNTY. Color plate, p. 37*

61 *FUR HAT. Dry brush, 1963, 15¾ x 23¼ in.*
     Lent by Mrs. Andrew Wyeth
*This is Adam Johnson. In the fall, when the artist returns from Maine, Adam greets him
with a bear hug and squeals of laughter. He refers to being painted as being sighted.
"He's sighting me. He's sighting me." Adam's farm on the side of a hill is very tidy. His
sheds and pens have been built from salvaged lumber, tied down with baling wire. From
a distance you can see his bundled-up, rotund figure moving back and forth between the
outbuildings, always busy at something.*

62   THE TROPHY. *Dry brush, 1963, 22⅜ x 30½ in.*
    Lent by Mr. and Mrs. Tate Brown, New York
For the last several years Karl Kuerner has made an annual trip to Newfoundland for
bigger game—moose. He leaves the farm in Young Karl's charge, drives straight through
to the last outpost, flies in to the area he has spent months reading about, shoots his
moose and comes directly home. Now the freezer is full with neatly wrapped packages
of moose meat and the rack of horns nailed to the side of the house he will show to his
German friends who come to call each Sunday.

63 *WASH BUCKET. Watercolor, 1963, 21 x 28½ in.*
Lent by Mrs. Thomas S. Kelly, New York
A bucket, gleaming like a polished helmet, hangs on the granary wall at the mill. Metal
buckets, pans, tubs, and cans glisten in and out of a great deal of Wyeth's work. He likes
the clash and bang of metal — the sound of sword against sword, the clank of a draw-
bridge gate, the echo from a jousting tournament. There is a sense of the medieval about
his work.

64 *RIVER BOAT. Watercolor, 1963, 17 x 26 in.*
   Lent by Miss Ruth A. Yerion, New York
Here we see the Brandywine and a landing just above Brinton's Mill. Tied up to the land-
ing is a barge or scow-like boat made by the owner. The Brandywine is a shallow river
ideal for canoes or boats of shallow draft. Coming by boat down the river you would see
many landings like this along the banks. In the spring this boat will be paddled or poled
down stream, tied to an overhanging limb, and Mr. Taylor will fish for carp and sunnies.

65 *DAY OF THE FAIR. Dry brush, 1963, 14⅞ x 19¾ in.*
     Lent by the City Art Museum of Saint Louis

*Kathy Hunt, seven years after she posed for "Granddaughter," sits pensively on a chair
in Wyeth's studio. She has changed from the sullen child into a very lovely young lady—
shy about posing. For weeks she had looked forward to the big event of the year, the May
Fair at the Chadds Ford school. When she arrived at the studio to pose, she had on her
best dress. Too polite to tell the artist that it was the day of the Fair, she missed the morning activities until he realized that the music coming from the direction of the school was
indeed the May Fair.*

66 *CIDER APPLES. Watercolor, 1963, 18⅞ x 24 in.*
   Lent by Mrs. Andrew Wyeth
*In this unfinished watercolor something of the frenzy and excitement that is so often sub-
merged after a painting is completed, clearly shows. Out of the chaos of swiftly applied
masses, an apple lying on the ground is clearly realized. Two other apples are just a faint
blur of color. It is as if all the glazes and overpainting had been removed and just the
underpainting remained.*

67 *THE DRIFTER. Dry brush, 1964, 22½ x 28½ in.*
Lent by Mrs. Andrew Wyeth

Out of nowhere Willard Snowden appeared at the studio one day asking for work. He had no intention of staying long—just needed to earn enough money to be on his way. Anxious to make a record of his fine head before he was gone, Wyeth started a pencil study. When he would look up from the drawing he would see Willard looking down at what had been drawn. The pencil study was abandoned, "The Drifter" begun. Willard decided to stay, and spent the winter in the studio.

68   *MARSH HAWK. Tempera, 1964, 30½ x 45 in.*
   Lent by Margaret I. Handy, Chadds Ford
The Wyeths moved into the newly restored house at Brinton's Mill in 1963. The hard
lines of restoration are in sharp contrast to the decaying buildings in "The Mill" of 1958.
The artist's friend Karl Kuerner had given him the large farm wagons which suggested
those that had rumbled up to the mill through the years. The late afternoon light catches
a marsh hawk on a stump near the falls and bathes the new frame wing in sharp contrast.

69 *MONOLOGUE. Dry brush, 1965, 22¼ x 28½ in.*
    Lent by Mr. and Mrs. William E. Weiss, Oyster Bay, New York
Willard Snowden, perfectly at ease, sitting in a chair at the studio. While he posed he kept
up a running conversation. He told of his travels with the merchant marine, of his wife
and daughter living somewhere, of the people he had worked for, of his life as a wanderer.
His voice is soft, never rising, flowing smoothly along like a slow moving river.

70 *UP IN THE STUDIO. Dry brush, 1965, 17 x 23⅞ in.*
      Lent by Amanda K. Berls and The Metropolitan Museum of Art, New York
Carolyn Wyeth, the artist's older sister, sits on a chair in her sparse studio. She is a
person with a powerful personality and her paintings show a brooding nature. A
woman absolutely devoid of pretense. The direct way she approaches life, cooking
a meal, gardening and painting, has always been admired by her youngest brother.
She is the one who stayed home — caring for her father's property with a fierce
devotion.

71 *THE COUNTRY. Tempera, 1965, 40⅝ x 35⅝ in.*
      Lent by the Virginia Museum, Richmond
Betsy looks out a window of the frame wing of their house. It's as if you took a
detail from the gable end of the house in "Marsh Hawk" and enlarged it. One
day she unexpectedly flung open that window to call to her husband. It was like
a cuckoo popping out.

117

72 *RIVER VALLEY. Watercolor, 1966, 21¾ x 30 in.*
    Lent by Mrs. Andrew Wyeth

Across the road from the mill is a vacant shell of a barn. One lowering winter day Wyeth climbed to the upper level and looked down on his land and buildings. Impressed by the dark browns of the river valley he started to paint. Then the grey clouds began spitting snow. Later he left the pad of paper propped up against the barn wall and walked home for lunch. When he came back the snow had drifted over the picture, slightly blurring the sky, which he left.

73 *MAGA'S DAUGHTER. Tempera, 1966, 26½ x 30¼ in.*
   Lent by the artist
A year later Betsy poses for this more formal portrait. There is a feeling of restrained elegance in the silk dress. Earlier the artist had always painted his wife with the feeling of outdoors. Clearly, in this portrait she is inside but she still wears a flat-crowned, broad-brimmed hat accented with two pale blue streamers. Despite the overall feeling of austerity, there remains a suggestion of slight amusement.

74   *GRAPE WINE. Tempera, 1966, 25½ x 29¼ in.*
    Lent by Amanda K. Berls and The Metropolitan Museum of Art, New York
Willard Snowden succumbed to his fondness for wine. One feels the succulence of grapes
throughout this portrait. A different man from "The Drifter" of 1964. Still living at the
studio he has become the official greeter. When strangers knock at the studio door hoping
to catch a glimpse of the artist they are greeted by Willard instead. He charms them with
his soft voice and glasses of sweet wine.

75   *FENCE LINE. Watercolor, 1967, 21 x 29¼ in.*
   Lent by Mr. and Mrs. Joseph E. Levine, New York
The side of the hill behind the house in "Brown Swiss" slopes down to the farm pond in front. The neat pile of rails alongside the fence will be used in the spring for fence posts. On the top of Kuerner's hill, Karl has planted a stand of pine trees. The wind has swept away an area of snow.

76 SPRING FED. *Tempera, 1967, 27½ x 39½ in.*
     Lent by Mr. and Mrs. William E. Weiss, Oyster Bay, New York
*When you enter Karl's milk room you hear the sound of running water. The water in this
trough comes from a spring in the side of Kuerner's hill across the road from the house,
the overflow spilling over the side of the trough. Through the windows of the milk room
one sees Brown Swiss cattle gathered in the barnyard where "Young Bull" was painted.*

77 HENRIETTE. *Dry brush, 1967, 22½ x 28⅜ in.*
     Lent by Patrick J. Leonard, Dallas, Texas
Henriette Hurd is the oldest of the five Wyeths. Each spring she tries to get back to
Chadds Ford from her ranch in New Mexico to paint the wild flowers she loves. Her
black eyes reveal the intensity of her nature and her quick mind. Devoted to her brother
Andrew, she enjoyed the period of being with him while she posed in a corner of his
living room looking out the window to the upper dam.

78 BAG OF APPLES. *Dry brush, 1967, 29 x 21½ in.*
Lent by Mrs. Marion Mann Hawkes
When Wyeth returns from Maine in the fall, apple picking helps to bridge the difference between the austere New England he has left and the lush fall of Pennsylvania. He enjoys just being in his father's orchard. Karl Kuerner will pick this bag of apples up and take it to the cider press.

79 FROSTED APPLES. *Color plate, p. 39*

80 FRENCH TWIST. *Color plate, p. 41*

81 HEAVY SNOW. *Dry brush, 1967, 20 x 40 in.*
Lent by Patrick J. Leonard, Dallas, Texas
Kuerners' under the weight of a blizzard. The building could be in Germany or in a Swiss valley. All the intimate things that are so familiar to the artist are buried in snow, but not for long. Before the picture was completed, paths had been shoveled, spruce boughs shaken, and roads cleared by Karl and his son.

82 OUTPOST. *Color plate, p. 43*

83 *MILLSTONES. Watercolor, 1968, 21 x 30 in.*
    Lent by Bailie W. Vinson, Tulsa, Oklahoma
Flung on the ground like giant stone discuses these millstones lie scattered beside the mill building. They are related to it. Only rarely has the artist placed an object in a picture that did not in real life belong there—the chalk parrot in "The Cloisters," and, possibly, the small figure of Margaret Handy in "The Children's Doctor." Wyeth will eliminate from, but seldom add to, a composition.

84 *SLIGHT BREEZE. Color plate, p. 45*

85 *GIANT JACK. Watercolor, 1968, 29 x 20½ in.*
    Lent by Mrs. James P. Mills, Middleburg, Virginia
Spring is lush in this river valley. Jack-in-the-pulpits grow to giant size. Skunk cabbages begin to show their horns poking through the bottom lands in early March. By May they have grown long, spreading leaves the length of an arm. Looking down on a mass of May apples is as if you were flying over a tropical rain forest. The woods the artist walked through during the winter months are now a tangle of undergrowth.

86 *WILLARD'S COAT. Dry brush, 1968, 29½ x 21 in. (framed)*
Lent by Nicholas Wyeth, New York
Many times Wyeth has painted Willard Snowden in this hooded coat.
Sitting on the ground in the orchard, walking across the fields, and
even in a blinding snowstorm. Not until he saw the coat hanging on a
hook in the corner of his studio after Willard had gone, did he do it
with any emotion. All that remains of Willard now is this coat and an
apple from the orchard. This is the same studio window behind Kathy
in "Day of The Fair."

87 *BUZZARD'S GLORY. Color plate, p. 47*

88 *BRADDOCK'S COAT. Watercolor, 1969, 27¾ x 18½ in.*
Lent by Mr. and Mrs. Edward B. McLaughlin, Easton,
Connecticut
Hanging from the tree on Christmas morning was this French-and-
Indian-War coat. Something about it suggested General Braddock's
defeat and death along the banks of the Monongahela. His officers
had ordered him buried on the road of retreat so that all traces of his
grave would be lost. Over this grave marched men, horses, wagons,
and cannons. Many years later when a new road on the approach to
Pittsburgh was being built, the grave, containing bits of red and blue
material from the General's uniform, was discovered.

89 *CIDER BARREL. Watercolor, 1969, 20¼ x 27¾ in.*
   Lent by Mr. and Mrs. Joseph E. Levine, New York
*One of the same wagons that appears in "Marsh Hawk." Wyeth found this barrel sitting
in the wagon when he came back from Maine. He never knew who put it there. It was
as if one of the many barrels in the mill marched down the mill stairs, crossed the field
and climbed up onto the wagon waiting to move off down the road.*

90 *RACE RUN. Watercolor, 1969, 33½ x 42 in. (framed)*
Lent by Mr. and Mrs. Robert E. Rann, Pleasant Ridge, Michigan
The frozen raceway leading into the mill is where Wyeth's hound, Nell Gwyn, loves to run. The cold must be prolonged and intense to freeze the water that flows swiftly along this race before entering the mill to turn the huge mill wheel. Now the raceway is locked in ice and Nell is the only swift movement.

91   ICE POOL. *Watercolor, 1969, 21½ x 29 in.*
    Lent anonymously
Here is a quiet pool of water surrounded by ice. Nothing ruffles the surface of the still
pool. However, the inky black of the water does make one wonder about the unknown
depth.

92 *HARD CIDER. Watercolor, 1969, 19 x 30 in.*

Lent by Mr. and Mrs. Carl A. Cantera, Wilmington, Delaware
Before the fourth frost Karl Kuerner descends into the orchard with baskets, quickly
gathers up all the windfall apples and takes them to the cider press. He brings home
three fifty-gallon barrels of sweet cider. Two of them are stored in his spring house, one
goes to Andrew Wyeth. When the cider begins to work, it is left undisturbed for a month.
The funnel is used to fill gallon jugs with hard cider which he carries up to his house.

93 *THE GENERAL'S CHAIR. Watercolor, 1969, 29 x 20⅞ in.*
Lent by Mr. and Mrs. Joseph E. Levine, New York
Betsy brought home a duplicate of General Washington's coat and
hung it over the back of a wainscot chair. All that was missing was
the General himself. He had been at this mill once, directing the line
of battle that day of the fight at Brandywine.

94 *MUDDIED UP. Watercolor, 1969, 41 x 29½ in.*
Lent by Mr. and Mrs. William E. Weiss, Oyster Bay, New York
Nell Gwyn curious but hesitating about investigating what might be
living in the hollow of a buttonwood tree. She is the second fawn-
colored hound Wyeth has owned. The first was Rattler. Wyeth likes a
dog that knows more about the land than he does.

95   *THE SWINGER. Dry brush, 1969, 14¾ x 24¾ in.*
   Lent by Mr. and Mrs. Joseph E. Levine, New York

*Johnny Lynch has a half brother, Jimmy. Here he is "watching the girls go by" from his front porch
swing. Jimmy is a watcher. He reports little happenings in the village. He rented this house right in
the middle of the town for a year or so. Night or day, rock-and-roll music poured forth from Jimmy's
house whether he was home or not. Ingenious at tinkering with things, he found a way to keep the
same record playing. The door was never locked — he never valued anything. But one day he reported,
"they stole my swing," and this made him mad.*

136

96 *ARABELLA. Dry brush, 1969, 13½ x 16⅜ in.*
    Lent anonymously

Mrs. Arthur Cleveland never forgets to leave a dainty basket of flowers at your doorstep on May Day. The flowers that grow around her house are haphazard and natural—a clump of blue flax, a sprinkling of snowdrops under the apple tree, a few daffodils near the woodpile. Everything she touches has this quality whether it be a trailing line of embroidered flowers or a thin butter cookie for tea. But one must not be misled by her delicate touch. There is a strength here that surmounted the loss of her husband, and her house at Lafayette's headquarters.

97 *MY YOUNG FRIEND. Tempera, 1970, 31¾ x 24½ in.*
Lent by Mr. and Mrs. Joseph E. Levine, New York
Sissy Spruance forded the river on horseback at Wyeth's mill. He would look out and see this figure, long hair flying, galloping bareback across his fields. One day sitting at a local lunch counter he met the girl. Now when he spotted her racing across the fields he could visualize her face. Keeping an eye on her for over a year, the time came to ask her to pose.

98 *DAM BREAST. Watercolor, 1970, 20½ x 29⅜ in.*
Lent by the artist
The water spilling over the dam at Kuerner's pond has frozen into an ice explosion. Just over the breast of the dam we can see the frozen pond—the same one that appears in "Brown Swiss." In the bare branches of the distant woods two crow's nests are silhouetted against the winter sky. The intimacy of Kuerner's is felt in this watercolor, a place the artist returns to again and again.

99 *AFTERNOON FLIGHT. Color plate, p. 49*

100 *LYNCH. Color plate, p. 51*

MAINE

102 *BLUE DUMP. Tempera, 1945, 27⅞ x 30 in.*

Lent by Mr. and Mrs. Philip Hofer, Cambridge, Massachusetts
The years spent at Port Clyde had been closely associated with the sea. Now Wyeth was
living in a more rural area, Cushing. People were farmers not fishermen. In a rocky
pasture where a path led to the spring sat this faded blue dump cart.

143

104 *WIND FROM THE SEA. Tempera, 1947, 18½ x 27½ in.*
     Lent anonymously

*Once the Olsons' had been a summer boardinghouse. The open third floor had been par-
titioned off into bedrooms. Climbing the staircase to this floor one hot summer day,
Wyeth found the rooms stifling. He walked to a window, opened it, and let in the wind
from the sea.*

106 *CHRISTINA'S WORLD. Tempera, 1948, 32¼ x 47¾ in.*

Lent by The Museum of Modern Art, New York (Purchase, 1949)

Andrew Wyeth saw in Christina a trace of the young girl he had never known. He saw in her struggle to move, a tall, thin girl who once moved swiftly. He knew she stayed back in silence. He paid her his highest tribute, "Christina's World."

123 *RIVER COVE. Tempera, 1958, 48 x 30⅛ in.*
        Lent anonymously

*The Georges River can be a turmoil of pushing waves. The wind can be blowing hard
but there is one cove, ringed by black spruces, that is so sheltered the wind never reaches
it. You can easily miss its entrance from the water. The tides have made a turn in and
out leaving a mound of sand. Herons fish here in the still water and leave their tracks on
the sand. The only sound is the rattle of a brook that empties fresh water into the head of
the cove.*

128 *WOLF RIVERS. Tempera, 1959, 13¾ x 13 in.*
   Lent anonymously
Sitting down one October day to begin a letter to his son Nicholas, away at school, the artist looked up and saw this basket full of apples catching the fall light. He made a quick drawing of it in watercolor on the letterhead and began: "Dear Nicholas." That is as far as he got. He went to the studio, found a small panel, and immediately began this tempera.

136 *DISTANT THUNDER. Tempera, 1961, 47½ x 30 in.*

Lent by Mrs. Norman B. Woolworth, New York

There was only one thing that would bring the Wyeths' hound Rattler back home during the day and that was thunder. During the many days Betsy posed for "Distant Thunder," lying in the field grass, she often fell asleep. Drawing quietly beside her one day, the artist looked up and was surprised to see Rattler asleep in the grass above. Then way off in the distance he heard the thunder.

158 *ANNA CHRISTINA. Tempera, 1967, 21½ x 23½ in.*
    Lent by Amanda K. Berls, New York

Christina never talked of the harsh reality that Alvaro was dying. After his death she wrote, "I knew surely but slowly that Al was failing, but as he never mentioned it neither did I." She became a wall of defiance as she posed each day. As he grew more frail she gathered strength to face her loneliness. When the horror fell upon her one cold November day, she woke to find the house cold. No one came. A day and a long night passed. When they did come, they found him wandering, lost in the rooms of that great house. They took them both away. She never saw him again. A phone call came to the Wyeths a month after his death. "Christina died during the night. We never heard her. The doctor said it was a broken heart."

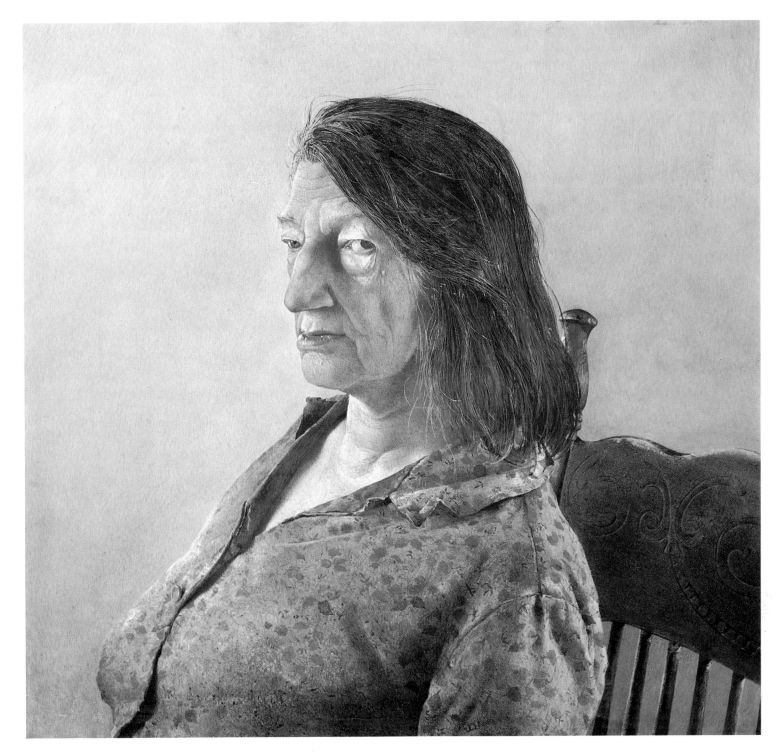

161   *ALVARO AND CHRISTINA. Watercolor, 1968, 22 1/16 x 28 1/16 in.*
       Lent by the William A. Farnsworth Library and Art Museum, Rockland, Maine
The auction notices had been nailed to the house. The relatives had sorted through
everything, keeping some, throwing away the clutter of years, and getting ready for the
big day. Wyeth raised a window and slipped in. He roamed through room after room and
finally found them in the two shed doors that led to the kitchen; Alvaro, the black door
on the left; Christina, the blue door on the right. A trace of the pink dress she wore is now
a discarded rag.

165 *BIKINI. Dry brush, 1968, 20 x 14 in.*

Lent by Amanda K. Berls, New York

Wyeth first became aware of Siri Erickson standing in a shed doorway gently stroking a cat in her arms. The tilt of her eyes, the slant of the cat's eyes, the suggestion of sullenness were there before him. It was late fall. In a few days he would be leaving for Pennsylvania. He might never have painted Siri when he came back the next June, if Olsons had not been over. Here his involvement is just beginning. This healthy young girl turns slightly back, before entering the dark gloom of the shed, to see who is passing by.

168 *END OF OLSONS. Tempera, 1969, 18¼ x 19 in.*
   Lent by Mr. and Mrs. Joseph E. Levine, New York
The broken windowpane on the third floor that was stuffed with rags in "Weather Side"
has been replaced. Looking out that window down on the toppling kitchen chimney, on
across the shed roof, we see the deep cove below. It was in this cove that Alvaro once
operated a fish weir. Here was where he anchored his Friendship sloop. Fall is in the air.
All but two swallows have left.

169 *THE FINN. Dry brush, 1969, 28¾ x 21 in.*

Lent by Mr. and Mrs. Joseph E. Levine, New York

George Erickson's bronzed head glistened in the morning sun as he stood in the same shed doorway as his daughter had in "Bikini." He is a man who has his own way of doing everything. When to plant his garden. How to fertilize the growing vegetables. How to benefit from the sun. How to raise his only child, Siri, to be strong, independent and self-reliant. How to live. No one will ever be ahead of him in the things that matter.

163

170   *SPRUCE BOUGH. Watercolor, 1969, 21¼ x 29⅜ in.*
       Lent by the artist
A snowstorm in Cushing came on the twenty-second of October — a rare privilege. The stone wall, the spruce trees, the pumpkins on the posts — all heavy with snow. The familiar suddenly transformed to a day in winter when the house would be closed and the artist gone.

101 *NIGHT HAULING. Tempera, 1944, 22½ x 36½ in.*
Lent by Mr. and Mrs. Burwell B. Smith, Palm Beach, Florida

In 1920 the Wyeth family spent their first summer at Port Clyde, Maine. The Anderson family were neighbors. While the artist was still in his teens he began using his closest friend, Walter Anderson, as a model. Days on end were spent to-gether on the water. Walt was the artist's most important link with the real Port Clyde, not the summer-vacation Port Clyde. In this tempera Walt, the poacher, is hauling a lobster trap at night. The water pours from the trap in a shower of phosphorescence. The phosphorous glow from the bait within the trap casts an eerie light on Walt's head, which is turned to listen for the approach of another boat.

102 *BLUE DUMP. Color plate, p. 143*

103 *CHRISTINA OLSON. Tempera, 1947, 33 x 25 in.*
Lent by Mr. and Mrs. Joseph Verner Reed, Greenwich,
Connecticut
This woodshed entrance was Christina's favorite spot to sit on a
warm summer day. It was just a step down from her kitchen.
She could look out onto her sweet peas and nasturtiums to the
estuary of the Georges River beyond. There would always be a
breeze from the prevailing southwesterly wind. The gnarled lilac
bushes had been planted by her grandmother Hathorne.

104 *WIND FROM THE SEA. Color plate, p. 145*

105 *SEED CORN. Tempera, 1948, 15⅜ x 21⅞ in.*
Lent anonymously
This is another of the rooms on the third floor at the Olsons',
across the hall from where "Wind from the Sea" was painted.
Being the driest place in the house, it made the best room to hang
corn to dry. The rats found it difficult to crawl across the line to
eat up the drying corn.

106 *CHRISTINA'S WORLD. Color plate, p. 147*

107 *THE REVENANT. Tempera, 1949, 30 x 20 in.*
Lent by the New Britain Museum of American Art, Connecticut
(Harriet Russell Stanley Fund)
There are sixteen rooms in the Olson house. Wyeth was free to roam
throughout. He could park his car behind the barn and start working
on a picture, and Christina would never betray his presence in the
house if someone stopped for a visit. It was their secret what he was
working on, and where. Returning home one afternoon from a day
on the water, he anchored his boat and walked up to the house to
check an effect he had been watching. Instead, he surprised himself
in a mirror of a room he had never been in before.

108 *BELOW DOVER. Tempera, 1950, 10 x 16 in.*
Lent by Mrs. Andrew Wyeth
Early that spring, "The Children's Doctor," Margaret Handy, had
taken the artist to lower Delaware where she had been born. The flat,
lonely stretches of waving marsh grass with the sea beyond had im-
pressed him. He went to Maine. There in a boatyard was a Friend-
ship sloop hauled out for the winter. The Delaware marshes, the
looming sea, the stranded boat became in the studio "Below Dover."

109 *SPINDRIFT. Tempera, 1950, 15 x 36 in.*
Lent by The Currier Gallery of Art, Manchester, New Hampshire
This picture, completed the same summer as "Northern Point," could be anywhere. A dory cast up on the shore like a long razorclam shell. Silver herring glisten in the bait bags, a swallow swoops around the empty boat. It seems as though it had just been beached and perhaps even had been drifting for a long, long time.

110 *NORTHERN POINT. Tempera, 1950, 36 x 18 3/16 in.*
Lent by the Wadsworth Atheneum, Hartford, Connecticut (The Ella Gallup Sumner and Mary Catlin Sumner Collection)
It makes no difference on whose roof this lightning rod sits. This is not a picture of an intimate spot. The point of land could also be anywhere, along any coast. This is like being at sea and charting your course by the sun. Or watching the needle of a compass point true North. It could be the center of the Universe.

173

111 TOLL ROPE. *Tempera, 1951, 29 x 11 in.*

Lent by Mr. and Mrs. William A. Worth, Greenville, Wilmington, Delaware
Wyeth's pictures in Maine are more symbolic than those in Pennsylvania. Perhaps he is
not quite so tied to location. Looking up the tower of a church steeple to the sky above
could be like being in the hold of a ship looking out the open hatch to the sky beyond.

112 MAN FROM MAINE. *Tempera, 1951, 20¾ x 20 in.*

Lent by Mrs. Stephen M. Etnier, South Harpswell, Maine
Forrest Wall is a certain kind of man you find in Maine. His philosophy is touched with
a keen wit. He holds an audience well. But under all the wit and charm is a man that
misses little in life. He walks silently in the woods. He knows how to graft trees. He
watches the road from his house and knows who is passing by. This day he moved
quickly to the corner window and peered out.

113 SEASHELLS. *Color plate, see jacket.*

114 *TEEL'S ISLAND. Dry brush, 1954, 10 x 23 in.*
Lent by Mr. and Mrs. Joseph E. Levine, New York

When it came time to do a portrait of Henry Teel he would not pose. So everything he touched, or placed, or used, took on a special significance. Because he lived on an island alone, the whole island became Henry Teel. This is a small boat he used to row out to his large power boat at anchor off the wharf. The house is beyond and on the roof is the lightning rod of "Northern Point."

115 *MARSH GRASS. Watercolor, 1954, 19 x 27½ in.*
    Lent anonymously
Time was running out for Henry Teel that summer. He had cancer. He was living with
his sister on the mainland at Port Clyde. The house on Teel's Island was closed. During
severe storms the waves break over the narrow strip of land and flood this marsh.

116 *TOMORROW THE OUTER SHOALS. Tempera, 1954, 19½ x 36¼ in.*
     Lent anonymously

Wyeth's brother-in-law, Sherwood Cook, lobsters for a living. The Cook family have owned windswept Green Island for several generations, maintaining the right to lobster off the surrounding shoals. Located on the mainland is the fish house where Cook repairs his lobster traps, stores his bait in barrels, and hangs from the ceiling freshly-painted lobster buoys to dry. Tomorrow at dawn he will load these buoys in his power boat, head for Green Island and use them to mark his traps sunk on the shoals.

117 *SOUTH CUSHING. Tempera, 1955, 27⅞ x 36¾ in.*
Lent by the Spring Hill Trust, Beverly, Massachusetts
The men of Cushing are proud of their horses. They travel for miles to attend horse-pulling contests at summer fairs. This horse had been put to pasture when Wyeth saw her and began making drawings. One morning he returned to find her owner had dressed her up with a harness and polished the brass for the occasion.

118 *BLEACHED CRAB. Watercolor, 1955, 13⅝ x 25⅝ in.*
    Lent by James Worth, Greenville, Delaware
This dried crabshell stranded ghostlike on the beach at Teel's Island looks like a knight
in armour.

119 *THE BED. Pencil drawing, 1956, 13⅜ x 19⅞ in.*
   Lent by Mrs. Andrew Wyeth
The occupant of this bed has just thrown the covers back and left. Her basket full of
letters, a Bible, a few pamphlets, are still there. She will be back. This is a drawing done
for "Chambered Nautilus."

120 *CHAMBERED NAUTILUS. Tempera, 1956, 25 x 48 in.*
Collection of Mr. and Mrs. Robert Montgomery, New York
Elizabeth James is back. She never will become completely bedridden. Her dashing spirit
will not allow it, even though her declining physical strength demands it. She was very
close to her son-in-law, the artist. They understood each other's natures. He caught a
little of her long-vanished youth and gave it back to her, and she gave him her daughter.

121 *HAY LEDGE. Tempera, 1957, 21½ x 45 in.*
    Lent by Mr. and Mrs. Joseph E. Levine, New York
Alvaro Olson should have been lost at sea. Maybe he really was. He gave it up to spend half a lifetime caring first for his father and then for his sister, Christina. He should have sold his dory but he didn't. High on the hay ledge of his barn he kept it freshly painted.

122 *UP RIVER. Watercolor, 1958, 20 x 28 in.*
   Lent by Mr. and Mrs. Alfred Bissell, jr., Wilmington, Delaware
There is a point up river where the Georges makes a swing and you lose sight of the open
sea at the mouth. The coves are sheltered from the wind, and a clam boat can swing
gently on its mooring. Pines grow right down to the water's edge. The clay of the clam
flats clouds the water.

123 *RIVER COVE. Color plate, p. 149*

124 *DRY WELL. Watercolor, 1958, 20 x 29¾ in.*
Lent anonymously

The pump in the Olsons' pantry drew water from a cistern below the floor. Rainwater
pouring off the high roofs above was fed by troughs and downspouts into this cistern.
For weeks on end no rain fell. Alvaro put a big barrel on a drag, towed it to the spring in
the pasture, covered the barrel full of water with a canvas and hauled it back to the house.
This was their well the summer of the drought.

125 THE SLIP. *Dry brush, 1958, 20 x 29⅛ in. (uneven across bottom)*
   Lent by Mrs. Andrew Wyeth

Rockland harbor is the last place you would expect to find a graceful Chesapeake schooner tied up to a wharf alongside a long coal shed. The harbor is lined with fish factories, heavy trawlers unloading their cargoes, and rotting wharves. It was like finding a racehorse in a slaughter yard.

126 ALBERT'S SON. *Tempera, 1959, 29 x 24½ in.*
   Lent by the Nasjonalgalleriet, Oslo

Jerry Stone lived with his nine brothers and sisters near the Wyeths in Cushing. His young mother had died the year before. His father, Albert, tried to keep the family together but after two years Jerry and his three younger brothers were sent to the Opportunity Farm. That last summer in Cushing he posed in the doorway of their barn.

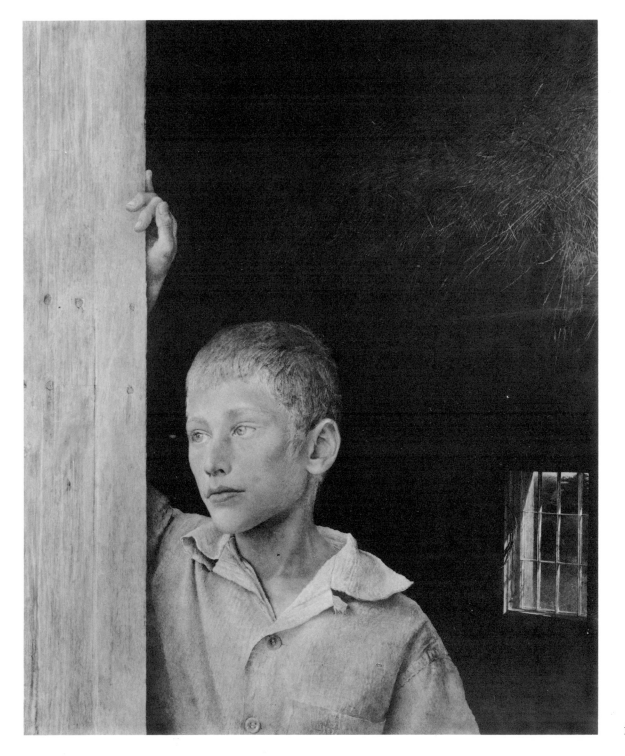

127 *FINN TOWN. Dry brush, 1959, 15 x 22¾ in.*
   Lent by Mrs. Paul J. Chase, Glen Head, New York
*The backbone of the community are the Finns. Once they worked
in the granite quarries, now they are farmers. Their stark frame
church sits on a rise of ground surrounded by cleared land. It is
an honor to have one call you his friend.*

128 *WOLF RIVERS. Color plate, p. 151*

129 *GERANIUMS. Dry brush, 1960, 20 3/4 x 15 9/16 in.*
   Lent by Mrs. Andrew Wyeth
*Standing outdoors at the Olsons' you could line up the kitchen
windows. In the near window is a white cloth thrown over the
dirty dishes, just beyond is Christina's head turned toward her
red geraniums on the far windowsill and the blue sea beyond.
Driving by you wouldn't see all this; but if you waved, a thin
arm silhouetted against the far window would wave back.*

190

130 PERPETUAL CARE. *Dry brush, 1961, 28 x 22½ in.*
Lent anonymously
This is the same church where ''Toll Rope'' was painted.
These ornate gravestones are like the spanking white
houses of Cushing with gingerbread mouldings running
across the porches and capping the windows. The faded
pink paper flowers suggest ''Christina's World.'' Death
is white to Wyeth.

131 BURNING OFF. *Watercolor, 1961, 29 x 23 in.*
Lent by Mrs. Norman B. Woolworth, New York
When this watercolor was started in Fred Olson's barn,
the bits and bridles alone emerged from the darkness of a
heavy fog. As the morning wore on the sun burned
through and the fog disappeared revealing the pasture
beyond.

132   *BERRY PICKER. Dry brush, 1961, 14¾ x 18½ in.*
  Lent by Mrs. Andrew Wyeth
Wyeth found his wife lying in the field above their house sound asleep. She had been
picking wild strawberries and had stretched out in the sun and fallen asleep completely
unaware that this drawing was being done. This is the beginning of "Distant Thunder."

133 *BROWN HAT. Watercolor, 1961, 11½ x 17⅜ in.*
Lent by Mrs. Andrew Wyeth
Here is the first drawing of Betsy's broad-brimmed brown hat. She wore it everywhere
that first summer it had been given to her. It would appear in "Distant Thunder," "The
Country," "Outpost," and "Hawk Mountain."

134 *BLUEBERRIES. Watercolor, 1961, 11½ x 17½ in.*
   Lent anonymously
This, as well as "Brown Hat," is one of the many drawings and watercolors made in
preparation for "Distant Thunder." The artist seems to follow no set pattern in the
number of pre-studies he makes for a tempera. Sometimes they are numerous.
Sometimes he will begin the tempera directly on the wood gesso panel without
making any preparatory drawings.

135 *SLEEP. Dry brush, 1961, 19¾ x 27¾ in.*
  Lent by Mrs. Andrew Wyeth
It was berry season. Each day Betsy walked through the fields picking. Wyeth
made drawing after drawing of her as she picked. The wild strawberry season was
over and now the blueberries were ripe. Still not sure the drawings would evolve into a
tempera, he made this very detailed dry brush.

136 *DISTANT THUNDER. Color plate, p. 153*

137 *HAWK MOUNTAIN. Watercolor, 1961, 21½ x 29¾ in.*
Lent by Mr. and Mrs. Halleck Lefferts, Washington, D.C.
The back hill country a few miles from Cushing. The figure of Betsy is sheltered
from the sharp wind by a huge boulder. We sense the top of a mountain we do
not see. She gazes intently through a scope. At what? A soaring hawk? A figure
on the granite outcropping at the top? A movement in the woods?

138 *BACK PASTURE. Watercolor, 1962, 23 3/4 x 18 15/16 in.*
Lent by the Cincinnati Art Museum, Ohio
Wyeth's dog had died. He cleared away some low-growing juniper and dug a
grave, leaving the pick and mattock leaning against a spruce stump.

139 WOOD STOVE. *Dry brush, 1962, 13¾ x 26¾ in.*

Lent by the William A. Farnsworth Library and Art Museum, Rockland, Maine

Christina sits at the table by the window in the room where she spends all her days. About ten in the morning she would crawl along the floor from her low cot in the living room, through the narrow pantry to her chair in the kitchen. Alvaro would have started the fire in the wood stove earlier, but Christina would keep it going through the day. She hitched her chair along to the woodbox by the rocker, grabbed a stick of wood between the palms of her hands, and inched her way back to the stove.

140   MAY 23rd. Watercolor, 1963, 22 x 30 in.
   Mr. and Mrs. Stephen W. Blodgett, Garrison, New York
Commissioned work is much too confining for Wyeth. The few times he has accepted a commission he has felt it cost him far more than what the picture cost the
owner—not in time spent, but in the invisible walls of restriction. "May 23rd" was
an exception. The Blodgetts had suggested that if he ever painted the church at
South Hope where they had been married (on a May 23rd), they could see it.
On his arrival in Cushing the spring of '63, the country looked alien. He wondered
why he had left the lush Brandywine Valley for this harsh land. Driving up to the

high country away from the coast, he found this carpet of quaker-ladies growing
in the churchyard. Not until he completed the watercolor did he realize he was at
South Hope.

141 *HER ROOM. Tempera, 1963, 25½ x 48½ in.*
   Lent by the William A. Farnsworth Library and Art Museum, Rockland, Maine
Looking through the uneven glass of the Wyeths' front windows is like looking from the
stern of a ship at a following sea. If the front door is open the faded taffeta curtains slap
in the wind. There is a feeling at high tide that any moment the sea will rise up and flood
the room.

142 *GEORGE'S PLACE. Watercolor, 1963, 21 x 30 in.*
  Lent by Mr. and Mrs. William E. Weiss, Oyster Bay, New York
Pumpkins are a fantasy to Wyeth. Before he hollows out the shell and cuts a face to leer
at him in the night, he enjoys just the twist of the stem, the waxy surface of the skin, the
shape sitting on a post in his backyard. George, a pet chipmunk, lives in the stone wall.

202

143 *OPEN AND CLOSED. Watercolor, 1964, 21½ x 27⅞ in.*
Lent by Mrs. Edward F. Hutton, Syosset, New York
This is the end of the room where Elizabeth James had posed for "Chambered Nautilus." Seven years later in this same room the artist spent day after day talking with her dying husband. They never alluded to death. Mr. James talked instead of the way the light hit this wall. The next summer, when Wyeth returned, the room was silent but the light was still there.

144 *THE PATRIOT. Tempera, 1964, 27½ x 23½ in.*
Lent by Mrs. Andrew Wyeth
To be a patriot, Wyeth found, a man must be tough. Certainly Ralph Cline is proud of his uniform. Proud of his World War I record and that he served his country the best he could. Proud to recite "In Flanders Field" at the Memorial Day services and to march in the parade. But all these things are only parts of his much deeper conviction: to be a patriot is to be on the alert every hour of your life for the smallest indications of the erosions of democracy. Cline screens this alertness with a very sharp wit and a jovial nature, but behind that screen Wyeth found the toughest man he ever met.

145 *THE WAKE. Tempera, 1964, 30 x 48 in.*

Lent by Mr. and Mrs. William E. Weiss, Oyster Bay, New York

That first clear, windy morning after Wyeth's arrival in Maine would haunt him the rest
of his life unless he did something about it. Circling wildly out of control was a boat
offshore. No one was in it. He and his son Jamie set out to find the missing person but the
madly circling boat led them off course. During the night Wyeth heard the heavy engines
as they dragged the river for the body. Pulled up high on the shore was the now quiet
boat with a few lobsters lying dead on the plank floor.

146 *THE PEAVEY. Watercolor, 1965, 21 x 29½ in. (framed)*
    Lent anonymously
The open door of Ralph Cline's sawmill. The peavey leaning against a birch log will be used to help roll the log onto the carrier in the mill. Sharp blades of the saw will rip the log into boards. It was in this sawmill, on the second floor, that Ralph posed for "The Patriot," looking out the back window onto a stand of spruces. Customers would come and go on the main floor below, never realizing that overhead Ralph and the artist were at work.

147 *SPLIT ASH BASKET. Watercolor, 1965, 21¼ x 29½ in.*

Mrs. Jérôme Rocherolle, Stamford, Connecticut

Alvaro Olson would not pose, but he is everywhere in the paintings done at his house. He is a pail full of water in "Weather Side." A dory in a loft of "Hay Ledge." A basket amid the clutter of his woodshed. Saying goodnight, his slight figure would be silhouetted in the kitchen doorway, the black shapes of that big house looming over him.

148 *WEATHER SIDE. Tempera, 1965, 48 x 28½ in.*

Lent by Mr. and Mrs. Alexander M. Laughlin, New York

It took Wyeth twenty-five years to paint this portrait of the Olson house. He had to know the room behind that window with the stuffed rags. He had to know the man who placed that pail of water on the ground. He had to know who was behind those red geraniums at the window. He had to know the life on the inside.

149 *STORM AT SEA. Dry brush, 1965, 19½ x 39¼ in.*
   Lent by Mrs. Andrew Wyeth

It was a raw day in September. A day to drive to Pemaquid Point to look at the lighthouse. Most of the summer crowds would be gone. The lighthouse sits on a bluff of land overlooking the open sea. Crowds gather on the grassy slopes all summer long to watch the pounding surf when the sea is running. Today it was deserted except for the gulls that had flown in from a storm at sea to perch on the grass under the shelter of the lighthouse.

150 *FAR FROM NEEDHAM. Tempera, 1966, 44 x 40½ in.*
   Lent anonymously

Most of the pastures in Cushing have long since been cleared of rocks. These rocks have made stone walls that enclose fields or divide property. Often walking through the woods you will come upon a stone wall and you know that once this was open land. When a boulder is too large to remove, it is left in place and used as a shelter for grazing sheep. These large boulders loom up like stone monuments on a village green.

151 FULL BUSHEL. *Dry brush, 1966, 24 x 18¾ in.*
Collection of Mr. and Mrs. Charles W. Engelhard, Far Hills, New Jersey
These blueberries have been raked, not picked. A hand scoop with a short handle and long tines placed close together is used for raking. At the end of day, baskets of these berries will be weighed on scales set up in the field. A truck will pick up the berries and transport them to a shed for winnowing. Then they will be sold to a factory for canning or freezing.

152 OPEN SHED. *Watercolor, 1966, 22 x 30 in.*
Lent by Bailie W. Vinson, Tulsa, Oklahoma
Years ago the last four-masted schooner sailed down the Georges River and disappeared forever at the island-clustered entrance to the river. Wyeth looked out and saw it pass. It was like one of the long white houses of Cushing all set with sails moving slowly down to the sea. Someone had left a cabin door open, or was it a door opening into a shed?

153 *GUNNING ROCKS. Dry brush, 1966, 18⅜ x 23⅞ in.*
   Lent by Mrs. Andrew Wyeth

*Walter Anderson has reached his mid-forties. He has remained as remote
as the Gunning Rocks where he and Wyeth used to roam as young boys.
These reefs lie south of Teel's Island. In a high sea they can be completely
covered by foaming waves. Sea birds, rafts of eider ducks, scoters and gulls
search endlessly for food around these rocks. It is a place, like Walt, that
has never quite belonged to the mainland.*

154 *CRANBERRIES. Dry brush, 1966, 18 x 12 in.*
   Lent by Patrick J. Leonard, Dallas, Texas

*There is a boggy area in the flat meadow at the head of Broad Cove. Here
in the fall cranberries ripen and turn soft if not picked before the first
frost. Two buckets, full of cranberries, sit on a table in the sun in the
Wyeths' dining room. These cranberries will go back to Chadds Ford and
be used for Thanksgiving.*

155 *THE SWEEP. Tempera, 1967, 25 x 36 in.*

Lent by the Flint Institute of Arts, Michigan (Gift of the Viola E. Bray Trust)

Starting at the Wyeths' house by the shore you pass through an opening in the stone wall. A pumpkin sat perched on a big post at this opening in "George's Place." This is where the crushed clamshell driveway begins. Just beyond the wall to the left below the spruce trees, Betsy slept in "Distant Thunder." A long, weathered steering oar lies on the wall this lowering day. The roadway winds through sweeping fields to the farm where the Jameses lived. The barn roof can be seen over the brow of the hill.

214

156 *ISLAND INN. Watercolor, 1967, 19⅛ x 30 in.*

Lent by Mr. and Mrs. Josiah K. Lilly, III, West Falmouth, Massachusetts
Jamie had left Cushing and found Monhegan Island. It had been a place Wyeth's
father had taken him to on day-visits as a child. Now his son planned to make it
his home. A five-mile stretch of open water separates Monhegan from the last
island. The light is different there. It is a light that separates you from objects.
There is a fine sea mist in between. At the turn of the century someone had built
a summer hotel that still flourished. On the front lawn boarders lounged in the sun,
but out back freshly washed sheets blew and billowed like small sails in the wind.

157 *THE SHOP. Watercolor, 1967, 22½ x 29 in.*
Lent by Mrs. Miller Chapman, New York
Charlie Stone was a gentleman-lobsterman. His fish house sits at the head of a cove on
the road to Mrs. N. C. Wyeth's at Port Clyde. It would never attract the artist looking for
the picturesque. No weathered boards or sagging roof. Mr. Stone kept his fish house
painted white and his lobster gear in perfect order. Tidiness runs in the family. Mr.
Stone has been gone for years, but his nephew, who inherited the property, keeps everything painted white.

158 *ANNA CHRISTINA. Color plate, p. 155*

159 *THE STANCHIONS. Watercolor, 1967, 19 x 28 in.*
   Lent by Mr. and Mrs. Mortimer Spiller, Buffalo, New York
This would surely be Alvaro Olson's last summer. His mind is wandering, his sad eyes glazed, his whole being frail. In his barn, from a rafter, hangs his blueberry basket. Long since the cow has gone, the dory on the hay ledge has been sold, and only thin cats slink in and out of his decaying barn; but the light coming through a window onto the empty stanchions remains.

160   *OFFSHORE. Tempera, 1967, 21¼ x 51½ in.*
      Collection of Mr. and Mrs. Charles W. Engelhard, Far Hills, New Jersey
*This was the summer of the fog. Unexpectedly this mysterious scow-like boat would
speed by and disappear into the fog. Or a fleeting glimpse would be caught of it going
the other way. What were these men doing? Where were they going? Who were they?
Then the fog lifted. They were clam diggers on their way to or from the clam flats of
Broad Cove, their coming and going dictated by the tides.*

218   **161**   *ALVARO AND CHRISTINA. Color plate, p. 157*

162 *ELWELL'S SAWMILL. Watercolor, 1968, 22 x 30½ in.*
Lent by Mr. and Mrs. Joseph E. Levine, New York

Ralph Cline knows every sawmill for miles around. One day he wondered if old man Elwell was still alive. As he and Wyeth turned down a rough dirt road that led behind a barn and through a wood, suddenly in the middle of nowhere was a saw-mill in the pocket of a hot summer valley. All was quiet. It could have been deserted but a team of horses were tied up in an open shed. Out of the shadows of the mill a small old man appeared. A man who had gone his way alone. When he took his money to the bank from the trees he had cut and hauled and sawed by himself, he owed no bills.

163   LOGGING SCOOT. Watercolor, 1968, 22 x 30¼ in.
    Lent by Mr. and Mrs. Joseph E. Levine, New York

*Elwell wasn't much for posing. He had watched his trees grow for years and now if he
timed it right he would get them all cut before he died. Every day he would drive the team
to his mill, walk back along his woods road and fell a few. Then he would walk back,
hitch the team to a scoot and haul the massive logs out to his mill. No reason for his sons
to get it all.*

164   *BLUEBERRY PIE. Watercolor, 1968, 29 x 37 in. (framed)*
   Lent by Mrs. Anne R. Trecartin, Miami, Florida
A pie has been put to cool on the same cupboard that the basket of apples sits on in "Wolf Rivers." The window that looks across to Wyeth's studio has been raised to hasten the cooling—the same window behind "Cranberries."

165 BIKINI. *Color plate, p. 159*

166 BAIT HOUSE. *Watercolor, 1969, 21 1/4 x 29 5/16 in.*
Lent by Frank E. Fowler, Lookout Mountain, Tennessee
Benners is an off-shore island where lobstermen spend the summer. They bring their families from the mainland to live while they lobster the waters around the surrounding islands. It is a dazzling blue day. The moorings swing empty. The men are off fishing but in the cool darkness of this bait house transparent fish scales glisten on big barrels full of salted bait.

167 THE PANTRY. *Watercolor, 1969, 30½ x 22½ in.*
Lent by Mr. and Mrs. Edward B. McLaughlin, Easton, Connecticut
Every room at the Olsons' has been stripped of generations of living. Somehow Christina's cookie jar sitting on the pantry shelf was overlooked.

168 END OF OLSONS. *Color plate, p. 161*

169 THE FINN. *Color plate, p. 163*

170 SPRUCE BOUGH, *Color plate, p. 165*

INDEX OF TITLES

Catalogue nos. in **bold face**, page nos. in *italics*.